The
Believer

CONFRONTING JEWISH SELF-HATRED

The Believer

CONFRONTING JEWISH SELF-HATRED

HENRY BEAN

THUNDER'S MOUTH PRESS • NEW YORK

Published by
Thunder's Mouth Press
An Imprint of Avalon Publishing Group Incorporated
161 William St., 16th Floor
New York, NY 10038

Library of Congress Control Number 2001097338

ISBN 1-56025-372-X

9 8 7 6 5 4 3 2 1

Interior design by Paul Paddock
Production stills by permission of Fireworks Pictures, Inc.
Printed in the United States of America
Distributed by Publishers Group West

Contents

Introduction

Henry Bean

I n October 1965, the *New York Times* received a tip that a young man arrested at a recent Ku Klux Klan demonstration in the Bronx was, in fact, a Jew. His name was Daniel Burros, he was twenty-eight, and lived in Ozone Park, Queens. Until a few months earlier he had been a high-ranking member of the American Nazi Party, but he had left the Nazis in a dispute with their leader, George Lincoln Rockwell, then joined the Klan, where, due to his considerable talents and industry, he quickly rose to become King Kleagle of the organization's New York chapter.

McCandlish Phillips, the reporter that the *Times* sent to interview Burros, was an interesting figure in his own right. An evangelical Christian, a lay minister who neither drank nor swore, Phillips was widely considered the best writer on the paper's city desk. Yet a few years later, and in part because of the Burros case, he would give up journalism altogether and devote himself entirely to the ministry.

The two met at a luncheonette located under the elevated train tracks in Queens. Burros laid out an articulate and surprisingly intellectual anti-Semitic argument. Phillips, after listening for a time, finally asked him how he could believe all this when he was a Jew himself. Burros at first denied it, but, when confronted with evidence (Phillips had proof that Burros's parents had been married in a Jewish ceremony), he told the reporter, "You print that in the *New York Times*, I'll kill you, and I'll kill myself."

The story ran on the front page that Sunday; Burros bought a copy out in Reading, Pennsylvania, where he was visiting Nazi friends. He came back to the house distraught, told them, "The *New York Times* says I'm a Jew." They wanted to talk it over, but Burros was inconsolable. He raced up to his room, put the overture to *Tristan and Iseult* on the stereo and shot himself. Twice. Once in the chest and, when that didn't work, a second time in the head.

Following his death, Jewish groups, readers and even some of the *Times*'s own staff criticized the decision to run the story. As a "Jewish newspaper," they felt, the editors should have understood that Burros was disturbed, possibly unstable, and that his threat was real. In response, the paper dispatched two of its rising stars, Abe Rosenthal and Arthur Gelb, to investigate further. They produced a book, *One More Victim,* that portrayed Burros's suicide as a product of Jewish self-hatred in the wake of Nazi genocide (the word "holocaust" was not yet in common usage). Burros, they argued, was a victim of Hitler, not of the *New York Times.*

The book traces Burros's progress from pious Hebrew-school student to rabid neo-Nazi, and the story is unsurprising: as a boy he was fair-skinned with a pug nose and took pride in not "looking Jewish." He went out for the high school football team, lacked talent, but revered the coach, who made casual anti-Semitic cracks, at which Burros dutifully laughed. He wanted to go to West Point, but no one took this seriously, and he was unable to get the congressional appointment needed to attend. After graduation he worked at menial jobs, read military history, decided Hitler was a brilliant strategist and began making pro-German anti-Semitic remarks to his mainly Jewish friends, chiefly to get a rise out of them. It worked: there were arguments, fights and ruptures. Soon his ideas had become even more extreme, but it had ceased to be a game.

Mark Jacobson, who grew up in Queens not far from Burros's home in Ozone Park, told me this story a decade later, proposing that we make it into a movie. We were living in Berkeley at the time, in that queasy interval between the end of school and the beginning of adult life, and we expended a good deal of energy imagining the films we would make without imagining very hard that we would actually make them. For this purpose, with its craziness, self-destructive fury and endless ironies, *The Danny Burros Story* was perfect. It seemed inconceivable that anyone would ever finance such a venture, but that not only didn't discourage us; we took it as evidence that we were on to something.

From the start we thought of the film as a comedy. A "Jewish Nazi" was seemingly absurd, and the Rosenthal/Gelb book, though largely predictable, contained one memorable detail: as a member of the American Nazi Party, and desperately concealing his origins, Burros would, nevertheless, bring knishes back to the Nazi barracks and date women who, according to his friends, were "obviously Jewish." The notion of Danny hiding his terrible secret and, at the same time, compulsively revealing it was fascinating and darkly hilarious.

Of course, to us, everything Jewish was funny. Jackie Mason used to get laughs simply by saying the word *Jew*. At times his entire act seemed to consist of little more than opening his mouth and pronouncing that one syllable, over and over, until the gentiles in the audience were looking at each other in confusion, while the Jews rolled around on the floor, gagging hysterically.

The hysteria came from the fact that Mason was proclaiming aloud, and with pride, a matter commonly viewed as an embarrassment. And even if he was overcompensating, that was part of the joke, for this mixture of vanity and shame was central to the business of being a Jew in America at the time.

After seeing an early cut of *The Believer,* the novelist Paul Hond said that it wasn't so much about a Jewish Nazi as simply about being Jewish. Which was, really, how Mark and I always thought of it. Danny Burros was our own Jewish ambivalence and hybrid Americanness exaggerated into comic proportions.

Even if we did not deny our origins and join anti-Semitic movements, even if we officially, perhaps even truthfully, liked something about being Jewish (though who could have said what) in the '50s and early '60s it separated us from an America that seemed otherwise uniformly calm, Christian and normal. We got into fights with kids from parochial schools, weren't invited to WASP cotillions, and had to have "our own" dancing classes and holiday parties. When we went to pick up a gentile girl for a date, we were sure that her parents were giving us an especially beady and mistrustful eye—even when, perhaps, they weren't. In junior high school, a friend told me that his mother had known immediately upon meeting me that I was Jewish, despite my innocuous name. He said this as if calling my attention to a mark on my face I might not have noticed, thereby wising me to the fact that I could never pass for a regular person. A thought that hadn't occurred to me because I could see that mark even better than his mother could. And had I missed it, my father would have been there to point out that Adolf Hitler, the ultimate authority in these matters, would have put me in a gas chamber regardless of what I might claim about myself. Clearly, being a Jew was not a matter of faith or testimony, as in a normal religion; it was inscribed into your flesh like numbers on your wrist. What a pointless redundancy those fucking yellow stars had been.

I want to stress that this youthful angst—though full of brooding, romantic longings, class-consciousness and the like—was hardly serious. It was nothing like being a Jew in a Russian shtetl, the Warsaw ghetto or an English public school. This was America in the age of television. Jewishness was just another identity crisis, a plot device, tougher than acne, simpler than homosexuality; Chuck Berry could have written a song about it. We just wished it would go away; or at least become invisible, shut up and leave us alone.

It didn't. It got bigger. I found it easier to imagine myself a woman than a gentile, I couldn't stop talking about "who was Jewish" and what was Jewish (butter, goyishe; mayonnaise, all Jewish), yet I could hardly have said what my Jewishness was, other than this sense of separateness, a "history of persecution" though, in fact, I had never been persecuted. It was an identity without palpable content.

In this it seemed a kind of hyperexistentialism; existence didn't precede essence, it *was* essence. To be Jewish, as far as I could tell, was to think of oneself as Jewish. Beyond that, I had no idea what it entailed. There was a religion out there somewhere, but, despite the usual bar mitzvah, I knew next to nothing about it. And though I enjoyed the paradox of this form without substance—like a mirror reflecting another mirror—it was frustrating. Above all, it accused me.

Of what? Of not knowing. Not knowing the religion, the history, the language, even, in much detail, the secular culture. I didn't want to know it, I wanted not to know it, not to be sucked down into that stifling ghetto of the mind. I looked at those people in their ugly black suits and white shirts, their covered heads and long skirts, their greasy hair, forgotten bodies, bad breath and worse politics. They were hideous, sexless, narrow-minded. But they knew. They knew and they knew, and in that knowing they didn't wonder what it meant to be a Jew. Therefore they belonged, not just to each other (which we, in our resolute individualism, never quite did) but to history, and, perhaps beyond it, to G-d.

Why would someone who seems to feel nothing for G-d, who neither believes nor doesn't, but for whom the whole subject is simply not an issue, why would such a person feel troubled by religion? Two possible answers: First, that he is lying to himself about his indifference, that all of life is that foxhole with no atheists (or even agnostics), that, as Simone Weil says, "We all have a hunger, even when we feed it by fasting." Second, that regardless of questions of belief, this particular religion links him to the traditions of his ancestors, which gives it an indispensable, even religious value. Maybe it was simply that, ignorant and disconnected as I was, I still felt the weight of history, conveyed through the great chain of Seders. If, as we said every Pesach, "it is as if I myself came out of Egypt," then presumably I myself had lived all of Jewish history; for thousands of years I had been saying the prayers, following the hallakah (the religious law), keeping this thing alive. And, if nothing else, I didn't feel qualified to break the chain. Yet the tradition held me without holding me. I stayed without knowing. And I broke the chain every day.

For years Mark and I did nothing about our movie. Back in that first flush of excitement, I had written a six- or seven-page treatment, laying out what has become, in fact, the opening scene, and following through to Danny's suicide. It was a Samuel Fulleresque tale, gritty, noirish and rather somber for what was supposed to a comedy. Mark knew someone who worked for Dustin Hoffman's company; we submitted it to them and never heard back. So we dropped it and went off about our lives, Mark to New York and I to Los Angeles.

In L.A., I met and then married Leora Barish, whose father was a Conservative rabbi and a career Army chaplain. Growing up on military bases and attending yeshivas, Leora had a Jewish experience shared by almost no one in the United States except her brother. She knew Hebrew, understood how the religion worked and couldn't help responding to the beauty of the biblical language. At the same time, she had had Judaism shoved down her throat, far more than she could swallow, and by then it nauseated her.

That combination of disgust and knowledge (plus a fetching indifference) made her the perfect teacher for me. She was, really, more a resource than a teacher; she had no interest in imparting what she knew and even less in convincing me of its truth or efficacy, since she had no use for it herself. You can imagine the seductiveness.

Yet when our son, Max, was born, Leora, who had previously eaten Chinese food on Yom Kippur, began almost without comment to attend a synagogue in Venice, California, where we were living. Sometimes I went along. Later I took a class on "Jewish meditation" and began reading a little on my own: Aryeh Kaplan, Rav Kook, the Tanya.... At night, in bed, I would read a *chumash* (the five books of Moses with commentary), going back and forth between the Hebrew and the English trying to puzzle out the original. Leora, lying beside me studying homeopathic repertories, would answer my questions about vocabulary and grammar and explain the *shoreshes,* the linguistic roots from which groups of words are derived, without looking up from her book.[1] Gradually, I began to appreciate the primitive power of ancient Hebrew, which I'd first felt when her father made the priestly blessing over us at our wedding.

Reading the Torah that slowly, a few verses a night, with digressions into the commentaries (little essays, often a thousand words or more on a single verse or idea), was like looking at an ordinary object through a microscope or on LSD. The complexity of the structures, associations and nuances overwhelmed me.

I realized that though I'd never read Talmud, nor had the first scrap of a real Jewish education, the thinking was familiar. I had been raised by a lawyer to be a lawyer, had spent years of dinner table conversations learning to climb around the jungle gym of legal reasoning. I had the typical American mistrust of "legalisms," yet those detailed, endlessly expansive, interconnecting discussions contained not only truth and beauty, but an emotional force that kept catching me by surprise.

Still, reading and thinking came much more easily than prayer and observance. I would emerge from temple each Yom Kippur glowing, serenely devastated, and promise myself a deeper practice in the coming year. And, a week later, watching Orthodox families walk to synagogue for Sukkoth, would feel only revulsion. I was nothing like these people. I didn't believe anything. How I could possibly practice their religion?

It was much later, after we'd moved to New York, that I decided it didn't matter if I "believed," whatever that meant. One could go to shul, light Sabbath candles and so on, not out of a conviction that G-d existed, much less that "He" actually commanded such actions, but for the actions themselves, the way they organized the day, the week, the year, for the pleasures of ritual, and to connect to and keep alive the traditions of one's forebears.

Later still, I read essays by the Israeli philosopher Yeshayahu Leibowitz, which made me doubt the very idea of a religion based on "human benefits." Leibowitz writes about actions done *Lishmah* (for their own sake) and not-*Lishmah* (for their effects). Though both have their place in religious practice, the former is clearly superior for it expects nothing in return. Leibowitz can barely conceal his disdain for a religion of efficacy focused on human needs, like my "pleasures of ritual" or the organizing of one's week. The purpose of religion, he argues, at least of Judaism, is man's service to G-d, not the reverse.

In Leibowitz I found for the first time a working explanation of Judaism that made sense. "The central aspect of 'Judaism'..." he writes, "has been the struggle over the Torah and its Mitzvoth..." That is the struggle to keep the commandments laid out by G-d in the Torah. These include not simply the original ten, but a vast system of laws and customs that, by rabbinic count, number 613. They cover not only typically religious matters, but also criminal and commercial law, torts, family relations, sexual conduct, treatment of disease and so on...

Leibowitz is bracingly contemptuous the impulse to adapt this system to humanistic ends. Speaking of a secular writer who wants Judaism to be about "'the satisfaction of a profound psychic need'" or the urge "...to be happier, more perfect, or moral," Leibowitz observes that all religions try to provide these things. What is specific to Judaism is the acceptance of "the yoke of Torah," and the observance of the *mitzvoth*. If doing this fulfills "psychic needs," or makes one happier or "more moral," that is largely incidental:

> Throughout his life [the religious Jew] rises early every morning *to observe the Mitzvah of prayer with the congregation* even when he feels no need to "pour out his heart before G-d," and perhaps has never felt such a need in his life. He may do so even though he knows that there is no need to inform the Omniscient of his needs and despite his understanding that as a frail human he cannot effectively praise and glorify the Almighty; he prays, it may be, contrary to his perception that there is no relation between his prayer and the events which befall him or occur in the history of Israel. If one day he or one of his children falls ill, he con-

sults the physician and resorts to the science of medicine as would any atheist, without diminishing the sincerity with which he recites the benediction "who cures the sick of his People of Israel."[2]

What Leibowitz is describing, and implicitly advocating—and from which I have borrowed heavily to inform Burros's thinking in *The Believer*—is obedience to the *hallakah* (the law), not because it "makes sense" or improves life, but because the Torah commands it. And he is careful to distinguish obedience from belief. One might believe in G-d, one might have seen miracles that attest incontestably to His existence and power, yet refuse to worship Him. (The Israelites who left Egypt saw the Red Sea parted, yet still made the Golden Calf.) Conversely, one might choose to worship Him without any evidence whatsoever of His existence. Leibowitz does not take the next step, but to me it seems inescapable: that one is fully capable of worshipping G-d (i.e. observing the *mitzvoth*) even when convinced that He does *not* exist.[3]

Here, at last, was a Judaism I could believe in, because it didn't require belief. It was beyond theology, beyond psychology, beyond reason. It offered nothing except itself, and therefore could never disappoint. Its very lack of argument was what persuaded me: that precisely by dispensing with all calculations of cost, benefit and truth, it offered something truly beyond this world, a *praxis,* things to be done entirely for their own sake. One might ask, then, why these particular things instead of others? And, unless you accept the divine origin of the Torah, there is no answer except that this system links you to a tradition and, thus, to your ancestors.

But in finding a Judaism I could believe, I realized something else: that I could never practice it. I could not accept the yoke of Torah, I could not rise early every morning to observe the *mitzvah* of prayer with the congregation. Maybe once a week, at best, and I doubted I could ever lay tefillin (put on phylacteries for morning prayer) or thank G-d for not making me a gentile or a woman—though, perhaps, I was grateful for both. I could not keep kosher or observe the Sabbath. I was too addicted to "the sweet joys of this life..." too busy, too self-absorbed, too greedy, too secular, too impatient, too fallen. I couldn't do it. I didn't want to do it, not enough—and this even though (abandoning Leibowitz's antiefficacy position for a moment) I was convinced it would be "good for me," for my family, perhaps even for the world.

It is interesting to discover that one cannot do what is in one's interest. *The Underground Man* says, "Sometimes a man does not want to do what it is in his interest. Sometimes he wants to do precisely what is not in his interest." But that was a protest against the crushing rationalism of modern life. I was refusing the very spirituality Dostoyevsky offered in its place. And, still, I couldn't do it.

One spring evening in the early '90s, Mark and I were driving around the New Jersey Pine Barrens doing research on a thriller we had been hired to write for Universal. Fifteen years had passed. Mark was now a well-known magazine writer and cult novelist; I had become a "working" screenwriter. And neither of us had written another word on the movie we still thought of as *The Jewish Nazi*. Yet when he blithely announced that he was certain we would one day make the thing, I concurred, though in my heart I didn't believe it.

I had spent the previous decade in Los Angeles, writing and failing to get made a handful of scripts that I loved and earning a living on others that I loved less. By now I dreaded every great idea that came my way; I had had so many and had completed so few, that each new one seemed simply a fresh torment sent to mock me with my inability to bring it off.

Yet here, driving through the April twilight, I couldn't resist a new scene for a film I hadn't even written: Danny Burros, the Jewish Nazi, takes a bunch of skinheads into a synagogue, intending to paint swastikas and plant a bomb. But, to his horror and disgust, he finds himself unaccountably moved, first by the sanctuary itself, the memories it evokes, and then, even more, by the ark, the Torahs, the mysterious calligraphy of the letters. The long-repressed Jew wells up in him. Suddenly appalled that he has brought Nazis into this sacred place, he tries to get them out of there, but before he can, one knocks a Torah to the floor. The holiest object in Judaism has been desecrated. Danny's heart is pierced.

Mark appreciated the lurid craziness of this scene, but he was uncomfortable with what seemed to him an excess of Jewish content. Yet that was why I liked it; I saw that in our earlier conceptions, we had made Danny Jewish without making him a Jew. But now imagining him as one gave the film new life. For weeks I couldn't stop thinking about it.

But then I went on to other things.

Mark and I have a mutual friend, Jonathan Buchsbaum, who teaches film at Queens College in New York. A couple of years after the conversation in the Pine Barrens, Jonny asked if either of us had an old, unproduced script from which his students could shoot a few scenes. Mark suggested we write some scenes from *The Jewish Nazi* and let them shoot that.

I began to write the interview between Danny and the *New York Times* reporter. Mark was tied up with work and family, so, in the end, I wrote all six scenes. The students had fewer skills and less drive than advertised, and we hired a professional cameraman, a novice production designer, picked up some amateur actors and I directed. The result (a year and a half later) was a thirteen-minute short called *Thousand,* after a Moby track we used over the opening scene.

In the course of this, almost without a conscious decision, it had become my film and not Mark's. This was due partly to his busy schedule, partly to my own greater involvement in film and Judaism, and, no doubt, to the infinite vagaries of personality. Jonny asking us for a script, offering equipment, crew and, above all, his own participation, seemed to me the opening of a door which, if we didn't walk through it, would close forever, and we would never make the film. I don't like to think that I stole Mark's idea, the idea he had first offered to share with me, but in some sense this is what happened, though less deliberately than that sounds. As Mark and I say in another screenplay—one we did write together—great deeds are often founded on a crime. And after nearly twenty years, doing anything at all with *The Jewish Nazi* seemed like a great deed.

Thousand was awkward and crude, but it had a power, and the central character was compelling. Encouraged by this and by the performance of a nonactor, Judah Lazarus, in the lead role, I quickly wrote a feature-length script.

When I began writing, I knew the story through the desecration scene, where Danny, against his will, begins to respond to the Torah. From there, it had to change, but it was not immediately clear how.

As a youth, Danny had hated being a Jew, so he'd become the opposite, a Nazi; the Nazis turned out to be boring and stupid, yet being one had brought him to a synagogue where his old self woke up and now urged him back toward the sweetness and piety he'd spent his life trying to escape, and which he still loathed, even as he loved it. I saw that Danny had to become a Jew again, but at the same time he had too much invested ever to give up being a Nazi.

Laying it out like that, the solution became obvious: he would lead a double life, resume Torah studies while, inexplicably, continuing his efforts to plant bombs and kill Jews. He would be a rabbi and a Nazi, a thing and its opposite, a living contradiction. He would not reconcile or synthesize the two; he didn't want them reconciled; he liked being pulled in opposite directions. This was irrational, yet felt exactly right. And it excited me like nothing I had ever written. It was the way I felt, not only about Judaism, but about so much else: America, my parents and myself. It seemed I had been looking for this story all my life.

"'I hate and I love'," Catullus writes in poem 85, "'and who can tell me why?'" I hate because I love, because I need the beloved and am therefore vulnerable to it. It can refuse me or betray me, and I hate it for this power it has over me. I hate it for the sweetness I feel toward it, the wish to merge with it, and the panic that it triggers (I will lose myself!) makes me push it away. I hate it because hate is the perfect complement to love, like peanuts and dairy, or boys and girls; they are incomplete without each other, and tastier and more beneficial together. Love without hate, with the hate repressed, was a dimmed and diminished thing.

To be honest, Danny's long bursts of anti-Semitic invective were the core of the script and the easiest parts to write. Most movies about ethnic or racial hatred are so embarrassed by their subject that do not invest the time and detail necessary to convey why the characters would feel such things. Similarly, depicting anti-Semites as rage-driven monsters or pathetic fools fails to explain or even wonder how it is that intellectually sophisticated and often brilliant minds have hated Jews and Judaism. But if we ask ourselves why, and if it is really a question and not a lament, perhaps we can come up with some tentative answers.

Here is one 4: Nazism was, among other things, a reaction against the dislocations of modern life. A number of major twentieth-century literary figures (Pound, Eliot and Wyndham Lewis among them) not only felt a similar anguish at these conditions, but were also attracted, at different times and to different degrees, to various forms of fascist anti-Semitism. (There are left-wing versions, as well.) Sifting through their distress at the breakup of traditional, homogenous societies, the ensuing "rootlessness" of modern life, the "degeneration of values,"[5] the coming of pop culture, and especially the rapacious spread of that greatest of all equalizers, money, or, better still, "finance"—it is not impossible to see how they could frame "the Jews"[6] for the job. For Jews seemed to embody modernity in their very being. If, as Jean Baudrillard has said, America was a post-modernist nation from its founding, the Jews have, in a sense, been post-modernists since Babylonian captivity. Long before Jacques Derrida, there was the Talmud, a de-centered, indeterminate text if there ever was one. After you have puzzled through those complex, infinitely allusive, hair-splitting arguments that somehow never definitively resolve anything, after you have followed the reasoning of why an injury inflicted by a man climbing a ladder requires a different remedy from the same injury inflicted by a man descending a ladder, after you have studied even a single page of Talmud with texts crowding in on and disputing with each other in radical nonlinearity, quantum physics, indeterminacy theory and floating currencies become, perhaps, less mysterious.

In this vein, I wanted Danny's anti-Semitism to be as sophisticated as possible, yet with an ironic edge so that each diatribe against the Jews would invert from a simplistic hatred to a mockery or dread of that hatred, even at times to an inadvertent celebration of the thing he hates. When he tells the gathering in Mrs. Moebius's living room that the public "will be glad" once they realize that Jews are being killed, is he saying that this is wonderful news for all of them as Nazis, or that it is the nightmare of his life as a Jew? He's saying both, and the horror and delight can never be disentangled. He tells the reporter that Jews believe in "nothingness without end," and sometime later a rabbi on television translates (actually mistranslates) *ein sof,* the most ineffable incarnation of G-d in Jewish mysticism, as "nothingness without end," as if no matter how hard Danny runs away, Judaism keeps catching up and pulling him back.

The very exuberance of Danny's invective tells us that something complicated is going on. As Carla says to him late in the film, "Oh, is that why you became a Nazi? So you could talk about Jews incessantly?" She's right; the speeches are his very life. He cannot stop talking about Jews. Hating them or loving them is finally beside the point.

But beyond this, I have to admit that I believed in those rants, not in their literal truth (if there could be such a thing), but in the sheer visceral pleasure of hatred. I got off on anti-Semitism, on the adolescent, Lenny Brucean pleasure of saying forbidden things. A Jewish Nazi who didn't enjoy his anti-Semitism, who was merely tormented by it, would make no sense; worse, he would be boring, and there would be no point in making a film about him.

More important, without an exuberant hatred I could never express my delight in being Jewish. The film is, finally, my love poem to my religion, my people. Jewish culture honors not only paradox and contradiction,7 but the spirit of self-criticism. This is commonly called self-hatred, but it is more than that. The comedy of a rabbi-manque who can praise G-d only by reviling him, love his people by despising and even trying to kill them, sounds like something out of a Hasidic tale or one of Kafka's paradoxes.

Yet I was afraid. I was afraid of offending gentiles and Jews, of being misunderstood, of being taken for an anti-Semite, or, should I say, only an anti-Semite. Above all, I was afraid of getting it wrong. My knowledge of Judaism is sketchy and self-taught. I read, studied, asked questions, had the script vetted by those who did know. But still I lived in dread of some dead-eyed yeshiva *bocher* with his twisted, sardonic mouth, someone who knew it backward and forward, casually pointing out the crucial thing I had missed, upon which the whole thing would fall to pieces at my feet.

It is odd to think of a movie being wrong. Maybe I was simply afraid that this love poem I was sending would be misread (A problem I'd had before). That like an Ionesco character, or someone with an eccentric version of Tourette's, I was trying to say "I love you" but what kept coming out of my mouth was "Fuck you."

In the initial showings in the United States, that had not happened; people seemed to get the movie and to like it. But as I set off for film festivals in Europe, where anti-Semitism wasn't just a conceit but a dark and terrible history, I worried that my "celebration" of hatred would look puerile and trivial.

I was going to festivals in three cities with special relationships to the film's subject matter: Moscow, the capital of a nation with a long tradition of anti-Semitism; Munich, where Hitler first came to power; and Jerusalem, which exists in its present form in considerable part because of what happened in the other two.

At the press conference in Moscow, the first question, asked in a dry

Russian-inflected drawl, was: "So, are you saying that Hitler and Goering actually loved the Jews?"

I laughed. I had never thought of it that way, but, following the argument, I could see how someone might come to that conclusion. It was, really, the kind of thing I would have wanted to say—blame everybody, forgive everybody—if I'd had the guts[8]

Yet just before I'd started shooting *The Believer*, a friend had showed me a Nazi propaganda film, *The Eternal Jew*. Made in the '30s, it is a loathsome work, intercutting images of Jews with those of swarming rats, and reeking with hatred, yet at times the film seems about to turn into something else. The word "Jew" occurs so often and the fascination, indeed, obsession with Jews is so unrelenting that one is tempted to say—as Carla does of Danny in *The Believer*—the only people I've ever met who were this interested in Jews were Jews themselves. At one point, a narrator tells us: "Only 2% of the population of Germany is Jewish, yet Jews comprise 38% of the lawyers, 46% of the physicians, 51% of the college professors." And one wonders, is this good or bad? Is the film complaining that Jews are taking more than their fair share of the top professions, or that they are, well, a master race? It is so difficult not to hear the second meaning like an echo behind the first that one wonders how well the filmmakers knew their own minds.

So if I didn't quite have the nerve to say that Hitler and Goering loved the Jews, surely there was a passion there, an obsession, that, if not love, was closer to it than would make us comfortable. Maybe we could imagine it as love unrequited.

Everywhere in Russia people made shrewd and intelligent observations about *The Believer*, and seemed to understand it perfectly. Yet there was an odd detachment, as if the subject had very little to do with them. The history of Russian anti-Semitism was acknowledged but never discussed. And, unlike everywhere else I've shown the film, very few people came up and identified themselves as Jews.

Part of that may be due to the odd nature of Jews and Jewishness in contemporary Russia. Someone told me that during the Soviet era being Jewish, even when not openly stigmatized (since Communists were supposed to believe in universal brotherhood), was invariably a professional disadvantage; therefore, many Jews married gentiles to dilute their problem, and perhaps to indicate a desire to be "real Russians."

As a result, though at first glance I saw very few Jews in Russia, on closer inspection, it seemed that almost everyone was Jewish. Or partly, or related to Jews or thought they were. It was as if one curious consequence of the deep-seated anti-Semitism was that the whole country had become hopelessly entangled with Jewishness (another Hebraic plot?), the ancient Cossack enmity now swirling around these aberrant Semitic corpuscles like the ingredients in an icebox cake.

As if, in short, it were an entire nation of Danny Balints. Which, since it was that old anti-Semite Dostoyevsky to whom I looked when writing, should hardly have been surprising. Danny's "inexplicable contradictoriness" wasn't shocking to the Russians, it was their national heritage.

The Believer showed twice at the Munich Film Festival, and after each screening, a vocal minority (Germans and Americans) argued that the film should not be exhibited to German audiences. It would encourage the neo-Nazis, perhaps give them new ideas and, worst of all, might allow them to claim that even the Jews know these things about themselves and are finally admitting it.

A larger but quieter group disagreed; they thought most Germans would find the film interesting, perhaps moving: a new way of looking at "all that." As for "the lunatics," they would never come to see it; in any case, they were beyond redemption, so it hardly mattered what they saw.

Behind this tactical disagreement seemed to lie a deeper issue: to the majority, the lunatics were a fringe element, repulsive but irrelevant; to the minority, they were the lurking, dreaded thing, always ready to return. Naturally, none of us worried about ourselves, our complicity in silence, our own fascist longings. We only worried about the others.

In truth, fascists were an audience I dreamed of and longed for. In making the film, I had had, among other grandiose notions, the idea that I was designing a cure for bigotry. Here, unlike in all the pious, liberal warnings against prejudice, was a celebration of hatred. Want to hear the words "fucking kike" declaimed joyously? Want to hear *why* they are fucking kikes? And yet as you watch (I told myself), it slowly changes. First, you realize that the one who hates Jews most and best is a Jew himself. Then you see that he is able to hate them only because he has studied them long and hard. The film argues that to hate a thing, you have to love it, too; to be a competent anti-Semite, you have to be a rabbi. What would the Nazis, the Klan, the Aryan Brotherhood, British neo-fascists and Hamas do with that? Would they confess that they loved the Jews? Or that the roots of their hatred lay in their own self-loathing? They would be turned against themselves. Even if they managed to hold onto their hatred—and, surely, it was too precious to let go of so easily—their grip would never be as sure. Or so I told myself.

In Munich, in all of Europe, the complexities of the past press in on you. The city in early summer was lush, beautiful and prosperous. The citizens seemed far more civilized, better educated and less susceptible to demagoguery than, say, their counterparts in the United States. As a German journalist assured me, if their election had ended as our last one did, the people would have taken to the streets in protest.

Still, it is hard to drop old prejudices. I had breakfast one morning with two men from the German film industry, then walked with them along the Isar River. With their almost unaccented English, their intelligence and easy wit, their relaxed, very un-Prussian manners, they were the furthest thing from one's clichéd notions of a German. Yet when it came time to ask them how to get to Dachau, I couldn't bring myself to do it. I didn't want them thinking: oh, the minute he gets here all he wants to see is a concentration camp (the Jew); no matter what we do, that's how they think of us.

I am sure that had I brought it up they would have answered exactly the way the manager of the film festival did when I asked her: she cheerfully whipped out a map, showed me which subway line to take and where to catch the bus, then, just to be nice, arranged to have someone drive me out there.

He was the same young Serb who had ferried me in from the airport when I arrived. He'd moved to Germany with his parents as a child and had grown up in Munich from the age of eleven. He alluded to a shadowy resentment toward the Germans, the sense of being an outsider, and, perhaps, an affinity with Jews since, historically, the Nazis hated us both. In this regard he mentioned that over on Shellingstrasse, an easy walk from the festival, was the beer hall of the beer hall putsch. Then he dropped me at the gate of Dachau.

Dachau was my second concentration camp. Twenty-five years earlier, a girlfriend and I had hiked up into Alsace to a minor installation used chiefly for prisoners from the French Resistance. Standing in the modest gas chamber, trying to feel something, we were surprised by a sudden burst of laughter. A busload of blond twelve-year-olds came screaming in and ran around like American kids at Gettysburg.

The experience disappointed me. I had wanted tears and horror, and had gotten happy schoolchildren. But Dachau was the real thing, it was supposed to be different. And for about a minute it was. Approaching along the side of the main building, watching my feet, the shadow of the wall falling across the raked gravel, I had to stop for a moment and thought: I can't do this, I can't go in there.

Then I turned the corner, saw the entrance to the museum, the crowds of visitors, and it was nothing, another tourist site. The historical exhibits, the rows of barracks, the cells for special prisoners, the ovens, the shrines of the various religions, it was all so much what you'd expect that it seemed like the Philip K. Dick concentration camp, a virtual construction providing perfect veracity and no feeling. "The horror" eluded me again, and though I have no idea what was going through the hearts and minds of the other visitors that day, I bet it eluded them, too. I didn't see anyone standing off alone, weeping or stupefied. And I had the unnerving thought that even if this had been 1943, it would have eluded us still.

Leora met me in Jerusalem. She had spent a summer on kibbutz as a thirteen-year old and hated all the Zionist propaganda she'd been force-fed, just like with the Judaism. I had never been and knew nothing, but of course I had opinions. I was an American; I believed in the separation of church and state. I couldn't accept that Jews, who for centuries had suffered under laws favoring one religion over another, would establish a nation the core of which, the Law of Return, did exactly that. I felt, also, some of the old Orthodox antipathy to Zionism as an idolatry of the land, a substitution of nationalism for religion.

But there were less logical reasons, vaguer, probably deeper. Like the "other" Phillip Roth of *Operation Shylock,* I was a diasporist; I liked exile, otherness, belonging in America, yet not completely; I liked multiple identities, but no definitive one, in short, the ambivalent, self-doubting, self-hating modern condition. So perhaps it was no surprise that my love poem to Judaism should have "fucking kike" as its refrain. Nor would it be a total shock if a nation of Jews not in exile and, presumably, not ambivalent, found this offering loathsome or irrelevant.

But they didn't. They were, I suspect, the best audiences the film will ever have. Even the ones who didn't like it liked talking about it. The question-and-answer sessions that at other festivals barely lasted thirty minutes went on here for an hour and a half and could have gone all night. They got every joke and reference; young men in kippot came up afterward explaining textual connections and allusions I not only hadn't intended, but that I couldn't really follow.

Best of all, they took Jewish anti-Semitism for granted. Everywhere else I'd gone, the inevitable question was "How did Danny come to be a Jewish Nazi?" In Jerusalem no one had to ask. Instead, they wanted to know had I made the movie about Israel? About the conflict between secular Jews and the ultra-Orthodox, which to many of them seemed more intractable and infuriating than relations with the Arabs. More than one person said that if the Palestinian problem were ever resolved, the Jews would then be at each other's throats the next day, and it would tear the country apart.

I had not been thinking of that when I made the film—I'd barely known about it—but, for a filmamaker, that it made them think of it seemed somehow to complete the whole project. They had taken my private obsession and made it their own, given it meanings, given it a life beyond what I knew or had experienced or, even, could understand.

The Believer was shot during June and July of 2000. Two weeks after we wrapped, the Democrats nominated Joseph I. Lieberman as Al Gore's vice-presidential candidate.9 It was the first time a Jew had run for national office on a major party ticket, and it seemed the perfect conclusion to an administration that had by its end a Secretary of State (sort of), Secretary of Defense (halfway) and Secretary of the Treasury (unequivocally) who were all Jews—or at least could be claimed as such.

This was partly a tribute to the Clintons, partly the result of broader developments. People who had gone to Ivy League schools in the 1960s had encountered large numbers of Jews who were not only bright and ambitious, but at ease in American society. And the '60s themselves broke down many of the remaining social barriers, so that by the time that generation reached positions of power, they had sat up all night bullshitting with Jews, gotten stoned and had sex with them, gone into business with them and by now were not infrequently married to them. In short, being Jewish wasn't a big deal anymore.

Was that good or bad?

While making *The Believer,* in which it sometimes seemed that the word "Jew" appeared more times than in any film in history—except, perhaps, the Nazi's *The Eternal Jew*—I often winced at subjecting a cast and crew of gentiles to my obsession, or perhaps at exposing the obsession to so many strangers. (Even now I wasn't up to being Jackie Mason.) Yet I never heard or even sniffed the faintest hint of complaint, discomfort or boredom at this monomania. As far as I could tell, no one cared.

When I say "the gentiles," I was not, in fact, always sure who was what. Years ago I'd met a couple who claimed that they had been together for months before either one realized that the other was Jewish. ("Are you really? So am I!") They weren't hiding it; it just hadn't come up. This had seemed inconceivable to me. How could you spend an hour in someone's company—much less have ongoing sex with them—without ascertaining that particular fact? Yet now I found myself wondering vaguely whether the gaffer or the camera assistant were Jewish, yet, strangely, not asking. Them or anyone else. I'd gossip about who might be gay or sleeping with whom, but not "that." Which can mean only that, strange to say, I didn't really care.

Somewhere in those weeks of finally making this Jew-obsessed work, of unraveling the idea that had defined me and which I was now trying to define, the subject itself seemed to be vanishing before my eyes.

We were free.

But what did it mean to be a Jew if it wasn't a problem? Without suffering (even the vicarious kind), what became of one's "Jewish identity"? If the Jews were free, if the oppression and the vast culture that grew up around it disappeared, if all the world ate bagels and no one at all ate kugel, then it seemed we had two choices: we could let it go at last and lose ourselves in the great sea of the nations, or we could perform the *mitzvoth.*

And then September 11th.

Then the Chinese jeweler told my friend Shirley (whom she didn't know was Jewish) that 4,000 Jews had failed to come to work at the World Trade Center that day (because they knew!) and that the FBI was treating the attacks as a Mossad plot. Then Peruvian cabdrivers and commentators on network television and guests at sophisticated dinner parties and patients with Jewish analysts were saying that it was because of Israel, because of AIPAC-funded distortions of American foreign policy, that at bottom it was again, as ever, the Jews' fault.

So maybe we weren't free after all. Was that bad or good? Because if the new, darker world scared and infuriated me, I could not deny that in some private room of the mind, it was also a relief. This was a world I knew how to live in.

Notes

1. Hebrew vocabulary is built up from three-letter roots called *shoreshes.* Recently I encountered the word galut, which is Hebrew but commonly used in English for the Diaspora. I asked Leora what it meant. Literally, she said, it means "exile," but it comes from the *shoresh gal,* "wave," and is associated with *galgal,* "wheel," as well as with *gilgul,* "rolling," and, also, "reincarnation," derived from the wheel of life.

2. "Lishmah and not-Lishmah" in *Judaism, Human Values and the Jewish Stat,.* Cambridge, Mass: Harvard University Press, 1992; p. 64. (emphasis in the original).

3. The philosopher Emanuel Levinas attempts to resolve this problem by arguing that in Judaism the law *is* G-d.

4. For others, see Israel Shahak, *Jewish History, Jewish Religion,* London: Pluto Press, 1994.

5. The phrase comes from an essay by that title interspersed in sections through the third volume ("The Realist") of Hermann Broch's trilogy, *The Sleepwalkers.*

6. "the Jews." The problem is the word "the"; it turns disparate individuals into a monolith, like the Borg on *Star Trek.* To say "Jews run Hollywood" is to make a factual claim (right or wrong) about a group of individuals. But "*The* Jews run Hollywood" implies that the studio chiefs, network heads and their ilk are acting in concert *as Jews,* presumably in the interests of the Jewish people. No one who has actually worked in Hollywood could imagine for a minute that these individuals act in behalf of anyone except themselves and, perhaps, their shareholders.

7. As they say: two Jews, three opinions.

8. One has to be careful talking about "the holocaust." The historical events remain unspeakable and incomprehensible and to make light of them in any way risks blasphemy. And yet if we are candid, and not just pious, then we must admit that we laugh about the terrible, we are bored by it and sick of it. We have heard too much and know that we've never heard anything at all and never will. One can see how the holocaust has become a kind of religion: like G-d, it is unknowable and would perhaps destroy us if we knew it. Yet we go on talking about it, seeking novelty, new abominations, ironic anecdotes, reversals of the usual oppressor/victim arrangements. We do this to amuse ourselves, to hide from what we cannot bear, to see it new and because, quite rightly, we believe that there is more to it than the official version and the keepers of the archives wish to tell us. There is always more, and to seek it—even in perverse forms, even if we know we know we'll never find it—is a mark of respect.

9. Lieberman's supposed appeal lay not only in his sanctimony (reprimand of Bill Clinton's moral lapses and his attack on the marketing of Hollywood films—also demonstrating a willingness to go after "the Jews") but on his own Orthodox Judaism that the Democrats hoped would appeal to the religious of all faiths. I have yet to see an analysis of whether he actually helped or hurt the Democratic ticket, though it is hard to imagine Gore having done so well in Florida without him.

The
Believer

The Screenplay

The text printed here is the final shooting script of The Believer *rather than a decoupage of the finished film. This will give anyone so inclined an opportunity to note the changes that the exigencies of production and editing have imposed on the original idea, and in my Screenplay Notes chapter (p. 183) I will note some of these as they occur. The Notes will also allow me to give a sort of half-life to scenes and ideas that had to be discarded in the brutal candor of making the film, but which affection and vanity prevent me from letting go of entirely.*

BLACK SCREEN

> RAV ZINGESSER
> "And God said to Abraham, 'Take you son,
> your only son, whom you love, Isaac, and go
> into the land of Moriah and offer him there
> for a sacrifice upon a mountain that I will
> show you....'"

INT. YESHIVA CLASSROOM—DAY

A run-down place. A dozen 12-year-old BOYS sit at old-fashioned desks. These are not Hasidim, but Orthodox Jews: normal American kids in yarmulkes. The teacher, RAV ZINGESSER is young, overweight, acnescarred, good-humored.

> RAV ZINGESSER
> And why did the Holy One—blessed be He—
> do this? Why did he ask Abraham to sacrifice
> his only son, whom he loved?

Two boys off to one side: AVI (a smart, tough, brownnose) and DANNY (the eternal dissident) argue under their breath....

12-YEAR-OLD DANNY
Isaac wasn't his only son. Ishmael was his son,
too.

12-YEAR-OLD AVI
The only son he loved.

12-YEAR-OLD DANNY
Oh, they only kill them when they love
them...?
12-YEAR-OLD STUART
(up front; answering Zingesser)
It was a test of Abraham's faith. Of his devo-
tion to God.

12-YEAR-OLD DANNY
It's not about Abraham's faith. It's about
God's power. God says, "You know how powerful I am? I can make you do anything I
want, no matter how stupid. Even kill your
own son. Because I'm everything, you're
nothing."

TITTERS. Danny looks around at his classmates: nerds, wankers,
nose-pickers. Two kids in back furtively read the racing form
under their desks. He hates them for their indifference as much
as he despises Stuart's piety or Avi's ass-kissing.

RAV ZINGESSER
But, Danny, if HaShem is everything, and we
are nothing how are we to judge His actions?

12-YEAR-OLD DANNY
We have free will and intelligence—which
God allegedly gave us....

                              AVI
Anyway, God never lets Abraham kill Isaac.
He provides the ram so that—

                      12-YEAR-OLD DANNY
Personally, I think that's a lie. I think he did
kill him.

                        RAV ZINGESSER
You think?! Based on what?

                      12-YEAR-OLD DANNY
There's midrash supporting this. My father
read a book by Shalom Spiegel that—Isaac
actually died and was reborn.

                        RAV ZINGESSER
No one follows that midrash.

                      12-YEAR-OLD DANNY
I do; I follow it. But okay, say God provided
the ram. So what? Once Abraham raised the
knife, in his heart it was as if he'd killed him.
He could never forget that. And neither could
Isaac. Look at him: he's traumatized, he's a
putz the rest of his life. By the end he can't
tell Jacob from Esau....

The kids laugh. Zingesser CRACKS a ruler against a desk.

                        RAV ZINGESSER
Watch your language....

                      12-YEAR-OLD DANNY
                    (rising impassioned)
I think the whole Jewish people were perma-

nently scarred by what happened on Mt.
Moriah, and we still live in terror....

> 12-YEAR-OLD STUART
> Fear of God is the beginning of wisdom.

> 12-YEAR-OLD DANNY
> Fear of God makes you afraid of everything.
> All the Jews are good at is being afraid. And
> being sacrificed.

Oooo. CRACK, CRACK, CRACK. Even the guys with the sports
page are shocked by that one.

> 12-YEAR-OLD STUART
> Don't you believe in God?

> 12-YEAR-OLD DANNY
> I'm the only one here who does believe. You
> say he's mysterious, yet merciful. I see him for
> the power-drunk madman He is. And we're
> supposed to worship such a Deity?? I say
> Never! I say...fight him. I say—

The ruler has been CRACKING from "power-drunk" on.... Now
Zingesser grabs Danny, yanks him out of his chair.

> RAV ZINGESSER
> Avi—ask Rabbi Springer to come remove
> Danny from the class....

Avi rises, grinning, as...Danny struggles wildly to get free.

> RAV ZINGESSER
> And you, if you had come out of Egypt, you

would have been destroyed in the desert with those who worshipped the Golden Calf.

                    12-YEAR-OLD DANNY
Then let Him destroy me now. Let Him crush me like the conceited bully He is.
                    (to the ceiling)
Go ahead. Kill me. Here I am. Do it!!

The class sits frozen in terror, waiting for God to kill Danny. But nothing happens.

INT. YESHIVA STAIRWELL—NIGHT

Danny runs down the steps alone.

EXT. RUN-DOWN COMMERCIAL AREA—TWILIGHT

Danny walking home alone. He sees TWO KIDS (older, tougher, blonder) coming toward him. He slips off his yarmulke and slants across the street. The kids slant that way. He hears a RUM-BLING, looks up at an ELEVATED TRAIN entering a station. He runs up the steps toward the SHRIEKING train....

INT. 7 TRAIN —1998—DAY

TITLE: 13 YEARS LATER

The train passes above used car lots, discount furniture stores, residential side streets...finally pulls into a station. The doors open. People file on, the CAMERA letting them go by until it spots a tall, thin COLLEGE STUDENT in a YARMULKE. Danny grown up?

PAN with him as he sits, opens an organic chemistry text. The doors close. The train starts up, but the Jewish boy hardly notices; he is already reading. He sways with the motion of the car, half-hidden by other passengers. We realize he is being watched.

REVERSE ANGLE: another YOUNG MAN, standing—a "SUEDE-HEAD" (his hair cut so short it's like a fine fabric).

SUEDE-HEAD'S POV: THE JEWISH BOY pushes his glasses back up his nose, wipes the nose with a handkerchief, puts the handkerchief away, and all the time his eyes have not left the page. Suede-head steps between passengers and stands directly over the Jewish boy. He looks down at the yarmulke pinned to the stiff, wavy hair, at the oversized shirt collar, scrawny neck, prominent Adam's apple, pimples, dandruff, ingrown facial hair...

He steps closer, crowding the boy's knees. The boy shifts a little without looking up. Subtly but relentlessly, Suede-head pursues him along the bench until, unable to slide farther, the boy flattens his legs against the seat. Suede-head presses into the boy's knees.

The boy accidentally bumps a BUSINESSMAN to Suede-head's left. The man (late 30s, *Wall Street Journal*, African-American) looks from the boy to Suede-head and understands at once what is going on.

Suede-head stares right back—and the BUSINESSMAN returns to his paper. Suede-head eases him aside and steps on the boy's shoe.

SHOES—A HEAVY BLACK BOOT PINS A BROWN WINGTIP TO THE FLOOR

The wingtip wiggles back and forth, finally working free. The boy still hasn't looked up.

SUEDE-HEAD & THE JEWISH BOY

swaying, locked in a strange, silent intimacy. Suede-head forces the boy into ever more contorted postures, increasingly ridiculous denials of what is happening. And the boy not only never stops reading the chemistry text, he keeps highlighting relevant passages.

The train slows. The boy closes the book, caps the highlighter, gathers his things and manages to stand up, wriggling awkwardly around Suede-head. The doors open, he gets off.

INT. STATION—DAY

Looking up a long escalator, the Jewish boy riding down toward us.

Suede-head arrives on the run at the top, races down a flight of stairs, vaults the bannister, slides down a metal slope....

Lands on his feet and comes to stand at the foot of the escalator.

The boy rides inexorably down. At the bottom, he tries to go around Suede-head who blocks this way, then another, driving him into a corner.

The boy realizes he has nowhere to go—finally turns to face his tormentor. Their eyes meet for the first time. He is actually bigger than Suede-head, but not nearly as strong. He won't fight, is simply acknowledging what he can no longer deny. There is even an odd relief that disgusts Suede-head more than all the rest.

SUEDE-HEAD

Fucking kike.

He slaps him in the face. He stumbles backward. As Suede-head goes to hit him again, the boy holds his books in front of him. Suede-head punches the books straight into his face. The boy falls, curls into a fetal position. Suede-head kicks him....

SUEDE-HEAD

Get up....Get the fuck up....

He won't budge. Suede-head punches him repeatedly until he hears VOICES approaching. He runs back up the stairs to the train and only as we FOLLOW him do we realize that he is our protagonist. This is Danny grown up.

CUT TO:

INT. DANNY'S STUDIO APARTMENT—NIGHT

Like his brain, the room is at once crowded and tidy and has, so far as we can see, neither windows nor doors. Shelves of books, CDs, magazines, videotapes loom over a neatly made bed.

Danny, in briefs and boots, is lifting weights. The phone rings. A machine picks up: no outgoing message, only a BEEP. Then:

> WOMAN'S VOICE
> Is this working? I'm trying to reach Danny
> Balint...Danny, it's Vicki, we met at Happy
> Jack's last month...?

He keeps doing curls.

> WOMAN'S VOICE
> I was hoping maybe we could...get together
> again....Give me a call—718-555-0193.

She hangs up. A moment later Danny finishes the set, gasping for air, heart pounding, muscles throbbing.

INT. SAME—NIGHT

A radio is playing the news. Danny sits at a small desk, on the phone and browsing the Internet, a take-out menu beside him.

DANNY (INTO PHONE)
...Is it completely vegetarian?...What do they
make the stock from?...
Not chicken, you're sure?...And no dairy...No,
no cheese I don't eat cheese...Yeah, all right.
And the tropical fruit shake...How long?...

Over this we see: COMPUTER SCREEN: GLIMPSES OF
PASSING PHRASES:

...ZIONIST OCCUPATIONAL GOV'T CONTROLS 78% OF
THE SENATE, 62% OF THE HOUSE...DYNAMITE CAN BE
STOLEN FROM CONSTRUCTION SITES & ROAD
CREWS, PARTICULARLY IN MOUNTAINOUS AREAS...
CURTIS ZAMPF IN NYC 5/18..JEWISH PIMPS, DRUG
DLRS & ABORTIONISTS HAVE AS THEIR MAIN GOAL...
CONVERTING THE GLOCK 901 TO FULLY AUTOMATIC
IS RELATIVELY SIMPLE. FIRST, REMOVE THE FIRING
PIN...

He HIGHLIGHTS the item about Curtis Zampf....

EXT. VOMPADINK—TWILIGHT

A tough working-class Queens bar.

INT. VOMPADINK—TWILIGHT

Men drink in clusters, including a group of skinheads....
Danny takes a place alone at the bar, drawing furtive attention
from the regulars. When the BARTENDER finally comes over...

DANNY
Vodka tonic.

A strange call for this place. As he waits, Danny turns and watches the skinheads enough to make them aware of him.

The girls watch him, too. The skins don't like that. One of them (Billings) seems ready to do something about it. The others try to calm him, and when they look back, Danny has left. He barely touched the drink.

The skins are puzzled, but one indicates his watch: time to go. They gather their stuff....

EXT. CITY/INT. 7 TRAIN—EVENING

Looking out the front of the train as it rushes toward Manhattan. A dramatic sky rises above the skyline.

EXT. STREET—NIGHT

The three skins—O.L, CARLETON, BILLINGS—walk up an East Side street. Billings is telling a story....

> BILLINGS
> ...So she takes the pants in back—where they try them on? And I think fuck it....

> CARLETON
> Are you shitting me?? Right in the store?

> BILLINGS
> She's been giving me the eye. She's hot. So I wait till the owner goes up front....

During this, O.L. starts to SPRAY PAINT a crude SWASTIKA onto a BUS KIOSK. A VOICE startles them....

                         VOICE
    What are you doing??

They jump, turn. Danny steps out of the shadows.

                         DANNY
                  (indicating swastika)
    What do you think you're doing?

                        BILLINGS
    Who the fuck are you?
                         DANNY
                  (coming toward them)
    Who am I?? Who are you, you schmucks, you
    can't even make a decent swastika.... Give me
    the paint.
              (O.L. looks to his friends)
    Give it to me.

Danny's will is stronger; O.L. hands over the spray can. Danny
shakes it, critiques O.L.'s rendering....

                         DANNY
                  (gruff but avuncular)
    It's too squared off. You got to orient it up
    and down, diamond-shaped, like this....
              (sprays an excellent swastika)
    ...The arms go clockwise.
              (hands the can back)
    You're going to Curtis Zampf; me, too. Let's
    go?

They exchange looks: how did he know about Curtis?

                   CURTIS ZAMPF (O.S.)
    ...Where I grew up in South Boston twenty

years ago, when a kid walked down the street,
everyone knew who he was...

INT. LIVING ROOM—NIGHT

Grand but threadbare. The skins enter: O.L. like a child, Carleton
like a sardonic adolescent, Billings like a revolutionary, Danny like
an uncrowned prince.

CURTIS ZAMPF is addressing a dozen or so guests. He is 40 but
appears younger; with rough good looks, longish hair and
a leather jacket, he seems more like an aging rock star or sexy novelist than a standard-issue American Nazi.

> CURTIS
> ...If he ran out in front of a car, some old
> Mick'd yell at him, "Jimmy Dunne, get back
> on that sidewalk and stay there...."

He does the Boston Irish accent so well, everybody laughs. Up
front we notice the only WOMAN in the room. She is in her 40s,
regal, beautiful, forbidding. Her name is LINA MOEBIUS.

> CURTIS
> ...The day he graduated high school, he'd go
> see his uncle down at the gas works, or the
> priest's brother in the shipyard, get his
> apprentice papers, eight years later he'd be
> making $16.50 an hour, have four kids, play
> ball on Sundays in Columbus Park, and when
> he died, the whole town'd get drunk and cry
> over him....

The crowd—nonunion electricians, white taxi drivers, unemployed
bookkeepers, failed academics, off-duty cops—listens quietly.

During this, a young woman (CARLA) appears from the rear of the apartment, heading for the kitchen with a coffee cup and a history book. She glances into the living room.

> CURTIS
>
> ...Today, when that kid walks down the street
> it's full of trash and half the faces are black.
> The shipyard's closed, all the jobs at the gas
> works are set-asides, and by the time he drops
> out of school, he can barely get a job at
> Burger King.
> So he drinks, smokes crack, and when he
> hangs himself on the front porch at twenty-
> three, the only people at his wake are a couple
> of buddies and his mother. The boy's father
> won't find out he's dead till six months later.
> (beat)
> The soul of this country is being destroyed,
> and all the government can offer is free trade,
> mutual funds and IPOs.

> GUY DANIELSEN
>
> You sound like a leftist.

> CURTIS
>
> I used to be one....No, seriously, I called
> myself an anarchist. I stood up for the
> oppressed. I opposed state power.

> AN OLD COOT
>
> Don't you still?

> CURTIS
>
> I oppose the present state because it's weak.
> It has been ever since the left emasculated it
> over Vietnam. But I think the average man is

crushed less by accumulated capital than by the loss of community or real leadership, the personal emptiness he simply cannot fill on his own....
(matter-of-fact)
That's why I'm a fascist. It's the only form of government that addresses our deepest needs.

Silence. Danny—who has spotted Carla—beings to clap, a few others join in. Danny raises his hand; Curtis nods to him....

DANNY
What do you think the fascism of the twenty-first century will look like?

Everyone—including Carla—turns to see who asked that.

CURTIS
More cultural than political.

DANNY
Obviously.

CURTIS
Decentralized, nonviolent, increasingly main-stream. We'll see antiabortion, anti-immigra-tion groups form alliances with the gun lobby, Christian identity types, tax resisters and even some libertarians....

The crowd seems impressed, but restless and bored.

OLD COOT
What about race?

A stirring: many share the concern. Lina watches closely.

                         CURTIS
          This isn't the time for that.

Murmurs of surprise, disappointment.

                         DANNY
          I disagree.
                         (glances at Carla)
          I think race is central to everything we're
          talking about.
                         (murmurs of agreement)
          Spiritual life comes from race. From the
          blood. Without that, we're no better than the
          Jews....

The magic word. The whole room comes alive. Zampf grimaces.

                         CARLA
          What's wrong with the Jews?

                      MRS. MOEBIUS
          Carla...

                         DANNY
          Have you read Toynbee? Spengler?

                         CARLA
          Nobody reads that stuff anymore.

                         DANNY
          Too difficult?

                         CARLA
          Too Christian. You know Jameson? Paul
          Virilio?

DANNY

The point is, the modern world is a Jewish
disease.

CARLA

Disease? What disease?

DANNY

Abstraction. They're obsessed with abstraction.

That stops the conversation. But Carla is intrigued; here is
someone whose mind moves in strange and interesting realms.

VOICE (GUY DANIELSEN)

What would you propose?

The questioner is young man (GUY DANIELSEN), better
spoken than the others. Danny feels all eyes on him.

DANNY

Killing Jews.

A tremor of fear and excitement ripples through the room. Zampf
glances at Mrs. Moebius; she is watching Danny intently.

CURTIS

That would be a catastrophic mistake.

DANNY

People hate Jews. Do you agree?

CURTIS

They used to. Today it's not an issue

DANNY

No, but deep down, beneath the "tolerance"

they learn on television, nothing's changed.
The very word makes their skin crawl.
            (around the room people nod)
It isn't even hate, really. It's more the way we
feel when a rat runs across the floor. We want
to step on it. Crush it. We don't even know
why. It's a physical reaction. Everyone feels it.

                    GUY DANIELSEN
Which ones would you kill?

                    DANNY
Prominent Jews. Who are either symbols in
themselves or who represent aspects of the
Jewish character people despise.

                    GUY DANIELSEN
Such as?

                    OLD COOT
Barbra Streisand.

Mutterings: "Who's she?" "Yeah, her..." But Danny says:

                    DANNY
Too obvious.

                    VOICES
Kissinger...Dershowitz...Roseanne...

                    DANNY
Yes. And Larry King...

                    OLD COOT
Is he Jewish?

DANNY

...Leona Helmsley, Michael Eisner, Bob Dylan,
Phillip Roth, Ruth Bader Ginsberg, Steven
Spielberg, Winona Ryder, Beverly Sills, Alvin
Toffler. Katherine Graham. All of them. But
not yet. We don't want celebrity obscuring the
issue.

CARLA

Which is what?

DANNY

At first, no one will know why the victims are
being killed.

CURTIS

You wouldn't announce it?

DANNY

I'd say nothing. After two or three, people will
try to find a pattern. A reason.

CURTIS

But when it comes out, the public will be outraged. It will look like Germany all over again.

DANNY

Isn't that what we want? Germany all over
again? Only done right this time...

The crowd feels a deep atavistic thrill. Zampf glances at Mrs.
Moebius....

DANNY

Without speeches or political parties. A

movement without leaders so that no one can stop it...

The room is stunned to silence. Mrs. Moebius signals Curtis.

> CURTIS
> Okay, let's break this up for now....
> (to Danny)
> Could you wait a minute...?

INT. SAME—FIVE MINUTES LATER

Danny—flushed with triumph—stands looking down at the city.

ACROSS THE ROOM—MRS. MOEBIUS & CURTIS ZAMPF

> CURTIS
> (low)
> ...I thought we agreed, anti-Semitism...it's exactly what we're trying to put behind us....Trash the blacks, fine; but...

> MRS. MOEBIUS
> Did you see how they reacted to him?

> CURTIS
> Yes, of course. But that only plays in this room, with people who aren't embarrassed to call themselves Nazis. If you want a modern fascism, you don't mention Jews.

> MRS. MOEBIUS
> It's a romantic movement, Curtis. It always has been.

> CURTIS
> Lina, the Thousand-Year Reich barely lasted a
> decade....Do you really want to go down that
> road again? In America of all places, where
> obedience and disipline are not exactly the
> national virtues...

She looks over at Danny, now chatting with Carla....

> LINA
> He's very bright.

> CURTIS
> He speaks well. But what do we do with him?

> LINA
> Let's find out who he is.

> CURTIS
> You mean who he really is.

ON DANNY & CARLA

> CARLA
> You're not in school? What do you do?

> DANNY
> I work at the Big Boy warehouse. In Queens.
> I drive a fork-lift.

> CARLA
> Where'd you read all that stuff?

> DANNY
> I just read it....

LINA
Young man...

He turns. She's beckoning to him. He gives Carla a look, then crosses to her, sitting in a chair she indicates. Curtis offers him a drink; he declines. Carla takes one.

LINA
Lina Moebius. And you are...?

DANNY
Daniel Balint.

LINA
Balint?

DANNY
It's German.

LINA (IN GERMAN)
What part of Germany are your people from?

DANNY (IN GERMAN)
From the Rhineland originally.

LINA (IN ENGLISH)
Are you with the FBI, Mr. Balint?...
Or any other law enforcement agency?

DANNY
I was going to ask you the same thing.

Smiles, laughter. Everyone seems to relax.

LINA
So what are you really after, Daniel?

...Do you just want to kill Jews, or do you have
something larger in mind?

Carla watches, silent. Danny is aware of both mother and
daughter.

> DANNY
> Without blood—a willingness to spill it—
> there's no real power, no authority.

> LINA
> (pleased by this)
> Curtis is afraid you'll marginalize us.

> DANNY
> We're already marginal. We are saying
> what no one else has the guts to say. Isn't that
> precisely our appeal?

> LINA
> So what Jew would you kill first?

> DANNY
> Ilio Manzetti...former ambassador to France.
> Managing partner at Damon, Schwarzchild.

> CURTIS
> (to Lina, explaining)
> An investment banking house.

> MRS. MOEBIUS
> He's Jewish? Manzetti?

> DANNY
> Totally. The family emigrated from Bulgaria
> when he was eleven.

CURTIS
How would you kill him?

DANNY
I'd have to research it, study his routines, his
security.... But ideally on a New York street at
midday, using a small-caliber automatic
without a silencer.

CARLA
Why no silencer?

DANNY
You want it to be an event.

Lina stands, takes a sherry. Everyone else rises with her.

LINA
Danny, why don't you come visit us in the
country. We have young men with lots of
energy and no ideas. Maybe you could give
them something to think about....Bring your
friends, if you like....

As Curtis leads him toward the door, Danny looks around for
Carla, hears WOMEN'S VOICES arguing in German. Frustrated,
he goes down the stairs....

EXT. STREET—NIGHT

Danny and the other skins walking down the middle of the street,
drinking beer, oblivious to traffic.
BILLINGS
Bring your friends.... We're not his friends.

DANNY
Then I won't bring you....

The others laugh. Someone HONKS behind them. Billings turns:

> BILLINGS
>
> FUCK YOU.

> BLACK VOICE (O.S.)
>
> Hey, bonehead...get your moon ass off the
> street.

Billings turns and throws his beer at the voice. A CRASH,
BREAKING GLASS, a screech of BRAKES, CAR DOORS open
and shut...

> BILLINGS
>
> Why don't you go back to Rwanda and give
> each other AIDS.

That does it. The skins run out of frame. SOUNDS of a fight.
Danny watches, indifferent, then finally joins in.

INT. PRECINCT LOCKUP—NIGHT

The skins in a cell. O.L., head bloody, moaning and vomiting.

> O.L.
>
> I can't see....

Carleton comforts him. Billings paces, looks at Danny, sitting
against the wall, relaxed for the first time.

> BILLINGS
>
> What, do you like it here?

> DANNY
>
> Read *Mein Kampf*? Hitler had all his best ideas
> in prison.

OFF-SCREEN VOICE
Daniel Balint?

Danny looks up: a JAILER unlocks the cell. Carla appears behind him. Danny stops without stepping through the open door.

DANNY
I'm not leaving without them.

The other skins are surprised, moved. Carla and Danny stare at each other. Finally she turns to the jailer....

CARLA
Can I use a credit card?

EXT. STREET CORNER, SUBWAY ENTRANCE— NIGHT

A Mercedes pulls up, Carla driving. The skins climb out, Carleton guiding O.L., who cannot see.

CARLA
He should go to a hospital.

O.L.
I'm okay.

Billings turns back, sees Danny still in the car.

BILLINGS
You coming?

DANNY
(glances at Carla, stays in the car)
We'll go to the country sometime, okay?

Billings nods grudgingly. The car drives off. Carleton grins.

>   CARLETON
> Fucking Danny, man...

>   BILLINGS
> He's an asshole.

INT. MOEBIUS APARTMENT—TWILIGHT

Carla leads Danny through the darkened apartment.

INT. CARLA'S ROOM—TWILIGHT

An old bookcase full of leather-bound German volumes...Danny opens one marked Hofmannsthal. He tries to read a marked passage.

>   DANNY
> *"...und die Worte zerfielen mir im Munde wie mod-*
> *rige Pilze..."*

>   CARLA
> "And the words fell apart in my mouth like
> moldering mushrooms..."

>   DANNY
> How come so many of the books are in
> Spanish?
>   CARLA
> They're my father's. He's from Argentina. My
> mother's family went there during the war.
> That's where they met.

>   DANNY
> Are they still together?

                    CARLA
He's in a mental institution....He's been there
for ten years, off and on. Mostly on.

                    DANNY
Is he a Nazi?

                    CARLA
I guess. His parents are. He doesn't care about
that.

                    DANNY
What's he care about?

                    CARLA
Killing himself.

They look at each other. There's that gulf between them that they
have to cross, but they're not sure how.

                    DANNY
You think people ever commit suicide out of
happiness?

                    CARLA
That's stupid. Why would they?

He shrugs. She takes his hand, rubs the bruised knuckles.

                    CARLA
You're not like the others, are you?... Your
friends.

                    DANNY
Yes, I am. Basically I am.

She leans close, whispers....

CARLA

Hurt me.

He's surprised, but not very. He grabs her wrist, twists it.

CARLA

Ow! That's too hard.

He pulls her out of frame. She starts to say something, but it's cut off by another CRY OF PAIN. We keep looking out the window....

INT. SAME—LATER

The light has shifted across the city, and we hear only a muffled sobbing.

The CAMERA TURNS to look at...Carla and Danny naked on the bed. He lies back, reading the German book. She's curled on her side, weeping abjectly. Still sobbing, she rolls over, buries her face in his chest. We see that his neck is scratched up.

CARLA

Do it again....

She begins to fondle him. He ignores it until he finishes the poem, then turns to her.

INT. SAME—LATER

The light has shifted again. Danny sleeps alone, his face strangely innocent. Carla drops onto the bed, shakes him.

CARLA

Get up...you gotta go.

He opens his eyes. She's dressed, her hair wet from the shower, a faint puffiness around her mouth. He pulls her down to him.

> CARLA
> No, you have to leave. I've got to write a
> paper.
>> (slaps his stomach hard)
> *Out!*

He looks up. Her face is cold, indifferent. He gets to his feet.

INT. MOEBIUS APARTMENT—DAY

Danny on his way to the door, hears something, turns...CURTIS ZAMPF is coming out of a bedroom in his underwear. From within...

> LINA MOEBIUS (O.S.)
> Bring the paper, too.

Curtis now sees Danny. A look between them. Danny goes out.

EXT. QUEENS, STAIRS TO ELEVATED TRAIN—DAY

Once a Jewish neighborhood, now occupied chiefly by blacks, Latins and more recent immigrants.

As Danny (wearing headphones) comes down the steps... TWO BLACK KIDS (big, menacing, boombox) are coming up, blocking his way. Danny walks right between them, forcing them apart.

They turn, glare after him. He turns, glares back. They scoff and keep going up. He walks on.

EXT. OZONE PARK HOUSE—DAY

He lets himself into a row house. We barely notice the mezzuzah on the door post.

INT. OZONE PARK HOUSE—DAY

A nearly vanished world of lower-middle-class Jewish life, though the "Jewishness" (menorah, kiddush cup...) is restricted to one dusty corner behind a secular chaos of books, newspapers, half-empty cups, half-filled glasses...

Danny's FATHER, 55, sits on a faded chair, an oxygen mask on a cart beside him. Danny's sister, LINDA, 30, is cutting his hair with a scissors. When Danny enters, they both look up at him in surprise, alarm, possibly even love. For a moment no one knows what to do.

The father begins to wheeze, puts the mask over his face and breathes deeply. Linda tells him to lean back; resumes cutting. On the wall we see Danny's BAR MITZVAH PHOTO.

Meanwhile, Danny has found a stack of mail, all addressed to him. His father and sister are visible behind him in a mirror. Without speaking, he goes down the hall, and we hear him DESCEND STAIRS to:

INT. HOUSE, BASEMENT—DAY

Danny has taken off his coat (revealing a black T-shirt with a red swastika), and is going though a number of cardboard boxes marked "D," pulling out comic books, baseball gloves, martial arts gear, drawings of voluptuous women, morbid gothic figures, gun magazines, books about Hitler, Nazis...and finally a .22 AUTO-MATIC stuffed in a blue sock.

INT. HOUSE, BASEMENT

He removes the clip, checks the slide, while nodding to the MUSIC coming through his earphones. He looks up, sees LINDA at the foot of the stairs, pulls off the headset.

> LINDA
> I knocked, you didn't answer.

It's too late to conceal he gun; he places it behind him. She does her best to ignore the swastika shirt....

> LINDA
> What are you doing here?

> DANNY
> I just came to get some stuff.
> I'll be out in five minutes.
> > (off her)
> He doesn't want me around.

She looks down as if that were not true, or the way in which it is were too complicated to go into.

> LINDA

> He's going to die.
> > (as Danny looks away)
> He won't take his medicine. He eats dairy. He probably still smokes when I'm not around.
> > (off Danny's helpless gesture)
> I asked him to come live with us. Alex offered to share his room, unsolicited.... But he didn't want to be any trouble.

DANNY
Then he couldn't be bitter about living alone.

LINDA
Why deprive him of his greatest pleasure?

They exchange what are almost smiles. But then the subject she's been trying to avoid—the only subject—suddenly erupts....

LINDA
Ah, Jesus Christ, Danny, how can you wear
that thing?... You know what it means? To
your people...

DANNY
They're not my people....

LINDA
Tell it to Hitler.

DANNY
Oh, he decides? Hitler's the chief rabbi now?...

LINDA
Is this because of those kids who used to beat
you up?

DANNY
What kids?...

LINDA
The Polacks? From Sacred Heart?

DANNY
Nobody ever beat me up.
        (as she sighs, turns to go)

Look, Linda, there're fifty reasons. Even if you
knew them all, there'd be another fifty you
didn't know.

> LINDA
> Do you know them?
> > (off him)
> I made him some noodles for dinner. You can
> heat them up and—

> DANNY
> I've got to get back to the—

> LINDA
> You can heat them up and eat with him.

INT. LIVING ROOM. QUEENS HOUSE—NIGHT

Danny (now wearing a plain white T-shirt) bends over the coffee
table eating a noodle casserole and reading the *Post*.
His father eats off a TV table. He finishes, cursorily wipes his
mouth, picks up a remote and turns on the television.

> DANNY
> It's Friday....

> FATHER
> > (a hoarse rasp)
> Do I give a shit?

Danny holds up both hands: he's not arguing, simply informing.

> FATHER
> The Torah says not to light a fire on the Sab-
> bath, because it's work, correct?

(Danny sighs)
But if alternating current's running through
the wires every second of every day, and I
throw a switch, send it here instead of there,
how is that lighting a fire?

                    DANNY
"Do chickens give milk?"

                    FATHER
Exactly.

He channel-surfs until he comes to a stand-up COMIC doing a
routine. They both watch.

TV: the COMIC is funny in a brutal, compulsive way. Lots of pop
references, implicit postmodern nihilism. The routine reflects
what Danny (and the Shiites, the Unabomber, Timothy McVeigh,
T. S. Eliot, et al.) have against the modern world.

                    FATHER
Who's this?

                    DANNY
Dennis Leary.

                    FATHER
Leary?

                    DANNY
No.

The father grunts with grim satisfaction, he suspected as much.

                    DANNY
              (offering consolation)
         Howard Stern.

                    FATHER
         Obviously.

Danny sighs: why bother. But adds...

                    DANNY
         Adam Sandler.

                    FATHER
         Funny?

                    DANNY
         Not like Mr. Dorfmann.

                    FATHER
         He was funny.

As they watch, apropos of nothing:

                    FATHER
         After your mother died, that's when you
         stopped going to shul. Doing your homework.
         Everything.

                    DANNY
         And that's when the Mets started to stink.

                    FATHER
         'Cause they got rid of Johnson. He knew how
         to deal with the assholes. Dallas Green,
         please...

                    DANNY
        Valentine...

The father snorts. On TV the comic gets off a line, and they both
laugh. Their laughs are quite similar; they glance at each other.

                    FATHER
        There's some maple walnut in the freezer.

                    DANNY
        Linda says you're not supposed to have dairy.

                    FATHER
        Just a little... What's the difference?

Danny goes into the kitchen. The father extracts a pack of Salems
from between the cushions, lights one, takes a desperate drag...
The phone RINGS. He curses, stubs it out, grabs the phone.

                    FATHER
        Yeah?...Hold on.... It's for you.

Danny gives his father a dish of ice cream, takes the phone.

                    DANNY
        Hello...?

                    VOICE
        Daniel Balint? My name's Guy Danielsen. I'm
        a reporter with the *New York Times.*

                    DANNY
                (impressed, suspicious)
        New York Times...?

His father looks up. Danny takes the phone into the kitchen.

VOICE

I'm doing a piece on right-wing groups, post Oklahoma City. I hear you're an important figure in those circles. You have a lot of interesting ideas....

INT. KITCHEN—NIGHT

DANNY

Who told you that?

VOICE

Isn't it true?

DANNY

No, it's...yeah, it's true, but... how'd you get this number?... No, not here... Maybe Sunday? There's a place off Queens Blvd. Near the courthouse...

EXT. COFFEE SHOP, QUEENS—DAY

A HIGH-ANGLE view of the coffee shop. After a moment, Danny enters frame, starts toward it....

INT. COFFEE SHOP, QUEENS—DAY

Danny enters, looks around. To his surprise he sees GUY DANIELSEN from the Nazi meeting rising, extending his hand.

GUY DANIELSEN

Danny...Guy Danielsen...

DANNY
(sardonic, now he gets it)

You...

Guy shrugs, smiles apologetically.

ANOTHER ANGLE—DANNY & GUY WITH COFFEE

>   GUY
>   Milk...?

As Danny declines, Guy gets out a small cassette recorder, is about to turn it on, when he notices Danny's reaction....

>   GUY
>   Is it okay if I record this?

>   DANNY
>   No... Yeah, fine, go ahead... So what's this
>   about? Is this about me?

>   GUY
>   I'm trying to figure out where the radical
>   right is going next....I thought you were the
>   most interesting person at that meeting.

>   DANNY
>   What about Curtis Zampf?

>   GUY
>   Curtis is a politician—and a bit of a hustler.
>   He's not a thinker.

>   DANNY
>   I agree.

>   GUY
>   The other night you said the modern world
>   was a Jewish disease. Could you elaborate on
>   that?

DANNY

In the movement—the racialist movement—
we believe there's a hierarchy of the races.
Not just in IQ, but in the civilization, the art,
the forms of government, the civilizations
that each race produces...Why are you writing
this down if you're recording it?

GUY

It helps me concentrate....So does that mean
you're a white supremacist?

DANNY

What should I be, a white inferior-ist? A mul-
ticultural Zulu egalitarian? Let me ask, where
are your people from?

GUY

My mother's family's French, my father's was
German, originally.

DANNY

German. Mine, too. So who do you think's
given more to the world, the Germans—
Beethoven, Goethe, Nietzsche—or the entire
continent of Africa? Ibos, Bantus,
Mandingos...

GUY

Danny, what about the Jews?

Danny shifts in his seat, growing more interested....

DANNY

The Jews are different.... Blacks are disgusting
and inferior, but it's like criticizing a retarded

child. The Jews are...a poison in the human
well....

GUY

A poison...?

DANNY

Let me give you an example....Sexuality.

GUY

Sexuality??? What do you mean?

DANNY

You ever fuck a Jewish girl?

GUY

What??!?

DANNY

Did you ever fuck one, Guy?

GUY
(laughing, embarrassed)
What's that got to do with...I've gone out
with a, with Jewish women. Why?

DANNY

And? What did you notice?

GUY

Notice? Like what...?

DANNY

Jewish girls like to give head, right?

GUY

I don't know. Is that right?

DANNY

And Jewish men like to get it.

GUY

Everybody likes to, don't they?

DANNY

Yes. It's very pleasurable. But the Jews are
obsessed with it. You know why?

GUY

Why?

DANNY

Because the Jew is essentially female.

GUY

Female...

DANNY

Real men—white, Christian men—we fuck a
woman. We make her come with our cocks.
But the Jew doesn't like to penetrate and
thrust—he can't assert himself that directly—
so he resorts to perversions. Oral sex is technically a perversion, you know that, don't you?
            (as Guy nods)
After a woman has been with a Jewish man,
she never wants a normal partner again. A
normal man.

GUY

Does that mean the Jew is better lover?

DANNY

You're not listening. He isn't better. He gives
pleasure, but that's actually a weakness.

GUY

Danny, what makes you think you know all this?

DANNY

Let's just say I've done due diligence.

GUY

So, fine, it's not that the Jew, the Jews own the
media and the banks. It's that they're sexually
corrupt.

DANNY

The Jews clearly control the media and the
banks. Investment banks, not the commercial
ones.

DANNY

But the point is they carry out in those realms
the same principles they display in sexuality.
They undermine traditional life; they deracinate society.

Danny leans over to make sure Guy's getting it right

DANNY

Deracinate...Tear out the roots. A people—a
real people—derives its genius from the land:
the sun, the sea, the soil. This is how they
know themselves. But the Jew doesn't have soil.

                    GUY
He has Israel.

                    DANNY
Those aren't Jews.

                    GUY
Of course they're Jews.

                    DANNY
Notice the Israelis: a fundamentally secular
society. They no longer need Judaism because
they have soil. The real Jew is a wanderer, a
nomad. He has no roots, no attachments. So
he "universalizes" everything. He can't
hammer a nail, plow a field. He can only buy
and sell, invest capital, manipulate markets.
He takes the life of a people rooted in soil and
turns it into a cosmopolitan culture based on
books, ideas, numbers. This is his strength....
            (pumped; this is what he loves)
Take the great Jewish minds: Marx, Freud,
Einstein. What have they given us: commu-
nism, infantile sexuality and the atom bomb.
In a mere three centuries since these guys
emerged from the ghettos of Europe, they've
taken us from a world built on order and
reason and hurled us into a chaos of class war-
fare, irrational urges and relativity, a world
where the very existence of matter and
meaning is in doubt. Why? Because it is the
deepest impulse of the Jewish soul to unravel
the very fabric of life until nothing is left but
thread, nothing but nothingness. Nothingness
without end...

                    GUY
Are all Jews the same?

                    DANNY
Differences exist, of course, but they're irrelevant. For the Jew, his Jewishness dominates
everything. Even the ones who renounce it,
who hate it, who want to cut it out of their
hearts with a knife...can't escape. They're still
just Jews.

Guy finishes writing that and looks up.

                    GUY
Danny, this is great. You're incredibly articulate. One more thing...How can you believe
this when you're a Jew yourself?

A beat. Danny smiles at the mistake....

                    DANNY
What? Excuse me?...
                    (Guy says nothing)
You're kidding, right?

                    GUY
Do you know Rabbi Stanley Nadelman? He
used to be at Congregation Beth Elohim in
Ozone Park...?

                    DANNY
Who? How would I know him?

                    GUY
He says you were bar mitzvahed there, in
March 1988.

DANNY

You believe that? And you call yourself a
reporter?

GUY

So you're saying it's not true.

DANNY

Look at me? DO I look Jewish? Look...

He indicates his hair, turns sideways to show his profile?

GUY

Were you ever bar mitzvahed anywhere else?

DANNY

Do you know who you're fucking with here?

GUY

That's what I'm trying to find out, Danny.
Who am I fucking with here?

DANNY
(sputtering, unsure what to say)
Listen to me....

GUY

Why would Nadelman lie?

DANNY

To discredit me. Because I know who they
are. Look, I thought I explained it to you.
Those people can say and do anything. And
they will. It's all narrative to them, it's... Are
you going to print what this guy said?

                              GUY

          Give me a reason not to.

                             DANNY

          It's slander. It's reckless disregard. I'll sue you
          and your fucking Jew paper.

                              GUY

          Does that mean you deny what he says is true?
          Yes or no.

GUN: pulled from Danny's pants, slammed down on the table...
Guy sits back abruptly. Danny picks it up, cocks it....

                             DANNY

          Look at me. Look at me, Guy....Oh, now you
          can't look at me? Look at me, you schmuck.
          Look at me....
                    (pokes the gun in Guy's face)
          You print that shit in the *New York Times*... I'll
          kill myself.

Everyone in the place is staring. Danny walks out, stuffing the gun
in his pants, shoving a man aside to get to the door.

EXT. COUNTRY—DAY

Traveling through low, tree-covered mountains listening to the
overture to *Tannhäuser.*

INT. VAN—DAY

Carleton driving; O.L. (one eye bandaged) riding shotgun. In back:
Billings and Danny (flipping through a *Times.*)

                    BILLINGS
Do we have to listen to this shit?

                     DANNY
Yes.

                    BILLINGS
Why'd we have to leave so fast?

                      O.L.
Nobody made you go.

                   CARLETON
Danny's running from the law.

                    BILLINGS
O.L., how come your mother gives you a car
when you're too fucking blind to drive?

                      O.L.
                   (cackling)
She says 'cause now I can't crack it up.

                   CARLETON
Hey, O.L., assholes at four o'clock.

O.L. leans out the window, giving dual "birds" to an empty street.

                      O.L.
FUCK YOU, ASSHOLES. SUCK MY DICK!

The others laugh.

EXT. DEFUNCT MOTEL—TWILIGHT

The van stopped in front. All of them out of the car. No one's around except the noisy CRICKETS. The city kids are uneasy.

> CARLETON
> I thought there were people here....

> DANNY
> I'll go look....

He walks toward the back. Billings decides to go with him.

> O.L.
> I better stay with the van....

> CARLETON
> Yeah, you better stay here and guard it.

O.L. gives him the finger. Carleton laughs—but he stays back, too.

EXT. REAR OF MOTEL—TWILIGHT

Danny and Billings see PEOPLE in back. Now NINE YOUNG MEN and a bulldog come to greet them: survivalists, speed-freaks. skinheads...and one blank loner (DRAKE) with a blue swastika tattooed to his lips like a tiny kiss. A case of STEROID EXCESS fixes his gaze on Danny.

> DANNY
> We're from New York. Curtis Zampf invited
> us.
> WHIT
> Who?... Curtis who?

Are they in the wrong place? Then someone laughs, they all relax, exchange greetings, obscure handshakes. Everyone's just getting comfortable when, for no apparent reason...

STEROID EXCESS

slugs Danny in the face.

He stumbles backward. The others crowd around, keep him from falling, also from getting away. Billings starts to help, but people grab him: this is Danny's problem.

Steroid comes at him....Danny steps inside the charge and goes to work on the bigger man's body. We barely see what happens, but we hear it and feel the crowd's shock. Danny is stronger than we realized and much more vicious. In seconds, Steroid sinks to his knees, face bloody. Danny holds him up, leans close:

>   DANNY
>   Enough?

Steroid mumbles in the affirmative. Danny nods—then hits him four more shots to the face. Even this crowd winces. Steroid drops with a wet thud.

As Danny straightens up, wiping the blood off his hands, people instinctively step back.

>   DANNY
>   Which was his room?

>   KYLE
>   (ferrety, glasses)
>   Number ten.

On the end: has an extra window. Danny walks into the room. Steroid's stuff starts flying out the door.

EXT. MOTEL PORCH—NIGHT

Danny on a pay phone

> DANNY
> Yeah, I'm trying to reach Carla, is she?...Did she get my other message?...No, I'll call back....

EXT. MOTEL PORCH—NIGHT

Danny hangs up the phone, glances into a room where we dimly glimpse Nazis taking drugs, drinking beer, screaming....

> VARIOUS VOICES
>
> Fucking niggers... Fucking niggers? Fucking gooks!...

Then incomprehensible shrieking rage, a fight, breaking glass...

Danny sighs, bored. He spots two nerdy Nazis, KYLE and WHIT, playing some battle re-creation board game and rehashing WWII....

> WHIT
> ...Look, if Hitler had knocked out the RAF in '39, which he could easily, easily have done, he'd have taken England, and the U.S. wouldn't have had—

> KYLE
> ...A staging ground for the invasion, yeah. But he blew it going after civilian targets. Just like

he blew the Russian front, diverting supplies
to Auschwitz....

Danny looks up the hill toward a farmhouse perched above them.
One light burns inside.

> DANNY
> Where's Mrs. Moebius?

> KYLE
> Her place is down the road. But she just
> comes out for weekends sometimes.

Danny squats to look at the board game.

> DANNY
> What is this, Stalingrad?

> WHIT
> Gettysburg. But we're refighting it with
> World War I technology. It's a fucking blood-
> bath.

He grins maniacally. Danny smiles. Kyle is emboldened by Danny's
unexpected friendliness, lowers his voice....

> KYLE
> That was unbelievable what you did to Lucas.
> The guy's an animal.

> DANNY
> You could do it.

> KYLE
> Get out of here....

DANNY
You look right through him. He's there, but
there's something on the other side of him that
you want. It's all you want. And whatever's in
the way doesn't matter....Then it's easy.

As Kyle and Whit contemplate this wisdom...

DANNY
Either of you know anything about explosives?

They both look up, very interested.

TWO FAMILIES IN TABLEAU—WOODEN CUT-OUTS—DAY

Jews: MAN (black hat, beard), WOMAN (sheitl, shawl), BOY
(kippah, twerpy), GIRL (fat, ugly), even a DOG, a Star of David
on its side.

Blacks: MAN (watermelon, pitchfork), WOMAN (fat, fried
chicken), BOY (syringe, 9mm), GIRL (twins, welfare check),
DOG (black).

VOICE (O.S.)
Take a breath, let out a little, relax, then
squeeze.

VOICE (O.S.)
(a RIFLE SHOT; nothing's hit)
Again...

Another SHOT. A bullet hits the Jewish boy in the rear end. Sunlight streams through the hole. We are:

EXT. REAR OF MOTEL—DAY

Danny peers down the barrel of an M-16. Kyle squats beside him.

> KYLE
> Which one were you aiming at?

> DANNY
> The mother.

Kyle nods, patient, is drawing Danny's attention back to the target when...

DRAKE

Sets up beside them, begins squeezing off rounds so fast, it sounds like an automatic weapon.

TARGETS: the bullets chew up and knock over all four Jews. And selectively: shooting the man's face, the woman's breasts, the boy and girl in the groin. The dog he merely flattens.

Drake looks at Danny without expression, drops the clip, shoves in a fresh one and riddles the black family in similar fashion.

EXT. MOTEL PORCH—NIGHT
Danny, pay phone to his ear, flipping through a *New York Times.* He throws it aside as a voice comes on the line....

> DANNY
> Carla?...It's me, Danny...Danny Balint...? We
> met at that...[meeting at your house.]

> CARLA'S VOICE
> Yeah, I remember.... Kill any Jews yet?

DANNY

I didn't realize you cared.

CARLA'S VOICE

I don't. I was just curious how full of shit you
were.

DANNY

Did you know that there was a *New York Times*
reporter there that night?

CARLA'S VOICE

Really, which one? I bet it was the guy with
the Prada shoes.

DANNY

I didn't notice his shoes....Did your mother
know he was there?

CARLA'S VOICE

I doubt it. How did you find out?

DANNY

He called me up. He wanted to talk to me
about my ideas.

CARLA

I bet. He didn't realize that nobody who talks
such a good game ever plays one.

DANNY

You weren't complaining about my play last
time.

CARLA'S VOICE

That's a much easier game.

                              DANNY
Why don't you come visit, we'll have a re-
match.

                              CARLA
Too many good players down here. I'm with
one right now.

                              DANNY
Oh, really?

                              CARLA
Bigger and better.

                              DANNY
Then how come you're talking to me?

                          CARLA'S VOICE
I'm not.

Click. She's gone. He hangs up, walks straight into...

INT. MOTEL ROOM—NIGHT
Nazis sprawled about, drinking beer, impassively watching TV.
The bulldog pants on the floor. Carleton calls to it:

                            CARLETON
Gas Chamber...

It trots over, receives a scrap of food. Everything desultory:

                              DANNY
                      (to the whole room)
When are we going to do something?

People glance up wearily: give us a break....

EXT. TOWN—DAY

Danny, Billings, O.L. and Drake walk through the town, looking for trouble. A couple of local TEENAGERS watch them, impressed by the swastikas, tattoos, swagger.

INT. DELICATESSEN—DAY

Two WAITERS (Jewish college students, athletic, confident) watch the Nazis come in. One indicates to the other that he'll handle this. He brings menus, water; he's carefully polite.

FIRST WAITER
You know what you want?

BILLINGS
We sure do.

The Waiter ignores the innuendo, readies his order pad.

BILLINGS
Ham and cheese on white.

FIRST WAITER
(forbearance)
We don't have ham. We don't have cheese.

BILLINGS
What the hell do you have?

FIRST WAITER
That's what the menus are for.

He smiles. Billings glares.

O.L.
Roast beef and Swiss.

FIRST WAITER

I said: no cheese.

O.L.

What's wrong with cheese?

FIRST WAITER

This is a kosher restaurant. We don't serve
meat with dairy.

DANNY

What about chicken?

FIRST WAITER

That's meat.

DANNY

The Bible only says don't seethe a kid in its
mother's milk. But chickens don't give milk.

FIRST WAITER

Look, you want cheese, go someplace else.

DANNY

But it's stupid, right? You admit it's stupid.

FIRST WAITER

No, I don't admit it's stupid.

DANNY

You can have chicken with eggs but not with
milk. Why is that?

FIRST WAITER

I'm not here to talk about religious law, if you
don't like—

DANNY
But you already talked about it: you said it's
not stupid. Why isn't it stupid?

FIRST WAITER
(calling the other Waiter)
Steve...

DANNY
Steve's going to explain it.

Steve approaches, a sawed-off broom handle over his shoulders.

STEVE
We have a problem here?

BILLINGS
We sure fucking do. We don't understand why
you can't eat chicken with milk. It doesn't
make sense.
STEVE
(an intellectual)
Religion isn't about making sense. It's about—

DANNY
It's about the incomprehensible, Steve, not
the idiotic.

STEVE
Fuck you.

DANNY
That explains it! Now we understand!

The Nazis laugh. Steve swings the broom handle at Danny...who
ducks it, grabs it, slams it back at him....GAVEL RAPS...

INT. COURTROOM—DAY

A JUDGE (white-haired, red-faced, blue-eyed, well-meaning) peers down at the four NAZIS, still bruised from the fight.

> JUDGE
> ...As the altercation appears to have been instigated equally on both sides, prison terms strike the court as excessive.

The Nazis are relieved. Spectators disappointed.

> JUDGE
> However, the defendants' political views suggest that they might profit from contact with members of our community whose experiences differ from their own....

INT. A SOCIAL ROOM—DAY

NUMBERS TATTOOED ON AN ARM...a thumb steadily smooths the skin as:

> RUMANIAN WOMAN (O.S.)
> (Rumanian accent, uninflected)
> ...When I refused to have sex with him, the warden had my sister, Esther, executed in front of the entire block....

The Nazis, accompanied by a "HATE COUNSELOR" (male) sit in plastic chairs opposite five elderly JEWS. The speaker is in her late 60s, still something of a beauty.

> RUMANIAN WOMAN
> ...Everyone considered it my fault. After that, of course, I did anything he wanted.

                    BILLINGS
        Why didn't he just rape you?

SNICKERING among the Nazis, a whispered crack:

                    O.L.
        Who'd want to fuck her anyway?

                HATE COUNSELOR
        I hear one more remark like that, we go back
        to the court for resentencing.

                RUMANIAN WOMAN
        He was a pig, like you, so perhaps he had no
        taste.

The Nazis laugh. The Jews try to calm the woman, though she has
spoken without any evident emotion. Billings gets up restless.

                HATE COUNSELOR
        Sit down, please.
                (as Billings sits)
        Thank you, Mrs. Cohen. Mr. Liebowitz, you
        indicated you had a story you wanted to tell....

INT. SAME—LATER

Nazis are dozing, staring out the window. O.L. threads a piece of
dental floss through the zipper pull on his trousers. Danny is vis-
ibly disgusted by the whole business. Over this we hear:

                POLISH MAN (O.S.)
        ...The man was afraid to let us hide on his
        farm any longer, but he agreed to take us to a
        more remote place. On the way he was
        stopped at a checkpoint, and when the

soldiers found us in the hay, one of them
grabbed my son out of my arms. He began to
cry, so I reached for him, not to take him
back, simply...

THE MAN: mid-70s, tall, stooped, a crushed spirit.

> POLISH MAN
> ...simply to assure him I was there. But the
> sergeant became enraged....He stuck his bay-
> onet in my son's chest, and lifted him up,
> impaled on it. My son was three years old....

Billings is muttering, "What a load of crap..." The Hate Counselor
looks over sharply. The other Nazis are stunned by the story.
Danny can barely contain himself, though we are not sure why.

> POLISH MAN
> ...He held him up so that the blood spurting
> out of him fell on my face....The soldiers were
> laughing.

FLASHCUT: EXT. A COUNTRY ROAD—DAY

A horse hitched to a hay wagon; FARMER driving. THREE NAZI
SOLDIERS have discovered a Jewish family hiding in the hay. A sergeant is holding up something unseen on the end of his rifle.

The Polish man who has been telling the story looks up at whatever it is. Blood falls on him. The Nazis are laughing.

> POLISH MAN (O.S.)
> When the blood stopped, the sergeant pushed
> my son off the bayonet and said, "There, you
> can have him now...."

BACK TO SCENE: INT. A SOCIAL ROOM—DAY

The room is silent. The Nazi faces blank, shaken. Until...

> DANNY
>
> And what did you do?

> HATE COUNSELOR
>
> What are you trying to say?

> DANNY
>
> What did you do while the sergeant was
> killing your son?

> BILLINGS
>
> Forget it, Danny, it's all bullshit.

> HATE COUNSELOR
>
> Wait a second...

> DANNY
> (to Billings)
>
> Shut up.
> (to man, mid-70s)
> What did you do?

> RUMANIAN WOMAN
>
> What could he have done?

> DANNY
>
> What could he have done?? You fucking
> kikes...

> HATE COUNSELOR
>
> You can't say that....

DANNY

The Nazi's killing his kid. He could've jumped the
guy. He could've gouged his eyes out, grabbed the
bayonet and gutted him.... What would you have
done if they were killing your son?

The counselor is briefly confused....

RUMANIAN WOMAN & OTHERS

...They'd have shot him on the spot....He
would have been dead in two seconds....Who
are you to judge?

HATE COUNSELOR
(to Danny)

Please sit down.

DANNY

SO THEY SHOT HIM! SO HE WAS
DEAD. SO WHAT. HE'S WORSE THAN
DEAD NOW. HE'S A PIECE OF SHIT...

COUNSELOR

Okay, that's it. You're going back to—

DANNY
(over him, to Polish man)

What do you think you should have done?

POLISH MAN

And you, you think you know what you would
have done? You have no idea. You can't even
imagine what that was like. And you never will....

Danny stares, momentarily silenced, but Billings is saying...

BILLINGS

Don't listen to them, Danny. It's all a bunch of crap.

ANCIENT JEW

What is crap?

BILLINGS

The so-called Holocaust. It never happened. It's the hoax of the twentieth century.

DANNY
(disgusted with this idiocy)
Oh, please...

BILLINGS

Danny, it's true. There were no six million. At most, two hundred thousand Jews died in the camps. And the majority of them were from disease and—

The Jews are shouting about historical records, the disappearance of families, whole towns.... But Danny is louder:

DANNY

Where did you read this? Robert Faurisson?

BILLINGS
(surprised he knew)
Yeah. He's a respected scholar. Even No-am Chomsky says he—

DANNY

Billings, if Hitler didn't kill six million, why is he your hero?...
Concentration camps all over Europe, and he

only gets rid of a measly two hundred thousand.... He's a putz.

Some surprise that a Nazi is arguing against a denier.

> ANCIENT JEW
> Hitler was not a putz. Hitler was real. God created him to punish the Jews for abandoning God.

The other survivors are embarrassed by this, but the Ancient Jew ignores them.

> ANCIENT JEW
> It is you who are putzes. Little pishas with your dreams of hatred and killing...

Danny scoffs, gets up to leave.

> HATE COUNSELOR
> Where do you think you're going?
> DANNY
> ...We have nothing to learn from these people. They should learn from us.

As Danny walks out, the Ancient Jew catches his eye.

> ANCIENT
> What should we learn from you, Daniel?

Her use of Danny's name feels knowing, slyly invasive. All SOUND VANISHES for a beat, and Danny barely manages to say:

> DANNY
> Kill your enemy.

EXT. MOTEL—DAY

Kyle opens the trunk of his car, shows Danny inside: two bags of shotgun powder and several lengths of metal piping with screw-on caps.

> DANNY
> What is it?

> KYLE
> Green dot—shotgun powder. For pipe bombs.
> (off Danny's reaction, smiles)
> A guy in a lumberyard gave it to me. A donation to the cause.

> CARLETON (O.S.)
> Hey, Danny....Guess who's here....
> (as Danny quickly slams the trunk)
> Your girlfriend... She's up at the house.

EXT. THE FARMHOUSE—DAY

In the driveway: Carla's Mercedes, a Triumph motorcycle. Danny peers in through the windows, goes to the door.

INT. FARMHOUSE, LIVING ROOM—DAY

Danny sees Carla sitting on a green sofa wearing a white sundress and leafing through a magazine. Curtis is mixing drinks. Lina is practicing with her stylus on a new electronic organizer.

> LINA
> My I's keep coming out as C's....

> CURTIS
> (spots Danny)
> The prisoner returns....

Danny greets them all. Carla barely looks up.

> LINA
> Danny, get a drink and come talk to me.

INT. LIVING ROOM—A FEW MINUTES LATER
Danny talking with Lina and Curtis but watching Carla.

> CURTIS
> ...Insulting people who were in the camps.
> ...What's the point?

> DANNY
> They're liars and cowards.

> CURTIS
> I'm sure they are. But what do we accomplish
> by pointing it out?

> DANNY
> It's the truth....

Curtis rolls his eyes. Lina signals him to lay off.

> LINA MOEBIUS
> Danny, what do you think of our troops?

> DANNY
> (trying to be diplomatic)
> They have guts. And they know what they
> hate...which is good. But they have no idea
> why; they don't think, they don't read....
> They're on beer and crank half the time....

A phone RINGS in another room.

                    LINA
          The young people in this country...They're
          like pigs; all they want is happiness.... But one
          needs pigs sometimes.
                    (as it RINGS again; to Carla)
          Liebchen....

Carla puts down her magazine, goes out to the kitchen. Danny's
eyes follow her, and Curtis's follow his.

                    LINA
          Do you feel you're making progress here?

                    DANNY
          You mean Ilio Manzetti?

                    LINA
          Forget Manzetti....Take on something simple.
          Something you can actually accomplish.
                    (to Curtis)
          Maybe he'd be more valuable in the city.

                    CURTIS
          An urban type.

Danny is stung. Carla calls from the kitchen.

                    CARLA (O.S.)
          Danny...telephone.

He starts: who could be calling him here? As he goes into the
kitchen to take the phone, Curtis says quietly...

                    CURTIS
          He's mad, Lina, you know that.

She hears him but doesn't respond.

INT. KITCHEN—DAY
Danny picks up the phone; there's a *New York Times* besides it. Carla busies herself about the kitchen.

> DANNY
> Hello?

> WOMAN'S VOICE
> You know what today is?

> DANNY
> Linda... How did you get this number?

> LINDA'S VOICE
> It's Mom's yartzeit.

Danny starts to hang up, sees Carla watching, turns away keeping his voice low.

> DANNY
> How did you get the fucking number?

> LINDA
> I want you to say kaddish for her. It's the only thing she asked from us....

> DANNY
> I don't do that.

> LINDA'S VOICE
> You do it on the inside....

                    DANNY
        Don't tell me what I—

                LINDA'S VOICE
        ...I want you to do it on the outside, too.

                    DANNY
        No!
                LINDA'S VOICE
        Yes!

He hangs up. He grabs the *Times,* looks through it quickly.

                    CARLA
        Who's Linda?

                    DANNY
                (dropping the *Times*)
        Why won't you talk to me?

                    CARLA
        I'm talking to you right now. Who's Linda?

He tries to kiss her. She pushes him away.

                    DANNY
        When can I see you?

                    CARLA
        You can't.

                LINA (O.S.)
                (in German)
        Carla, it's time to leave.

CARLA

I have to go visit my father.

DANNY

Your father??

CARLA

He's at a home out here.

She starts to walk past. He grabs her arm.

DANNY

I'm coming to your room tonight.

CARLA

No.

She tries to pull free; he won't let her go.

LINA (O.S.)

Carla!

CARLA

Just after midnight. Five past...But don't come through the house, they'll hear you. I'm in the back bedroom, second floor. Climb onto the kitchen roof, I'll leave the window open.

He tries to kiss her, but she ducks away and goes out.

EXT. STREET/INT. O.L.'S VAN—EVENING

Danny is parked opposite a fortresslike building of soiled brick. For a long time he cannot bring himself to get out. Finally he opens the door....

INT. AHAVAT TORAH, FOYER—EVENING

A LARGE WOMAN, about 40, her body barely contained by a brilliant magenta dress, greets him with a smile the size of a wedding cake. She holds out a prayer book stuffed with flyers.

> LARGE WOMAN
> Shabbat shalom.

She speaks quietly, not wanting to disturb the service, yet even so her voice is huge, and her flashing eyes clearly expect some kind of enthusiastic response. Within we hear the ALENU being chanted.

Danny ignores her and the proffered siddur. A basket of yarmulkes seems to infuriate him, but he snatches one anyway and, conveying a helpless disgust, puts it on his head. From within he hears...

> CONGREGATION (O.S.)
> (in rough unison)
> Ba-yom ha-hoo, ba-yom ha hoo...(etc.)

He stands with his hand on the door, but not opening it.

> RABBI'S AMPLIFIED VOICE (O.S.)
> On that day, the Eternal shall be One. And
> His Name shall be One....

The organist plays a brief decrescendo....

> RABBI'S AMPLIFIED VOICE
> The mourner's kaddish can be found on page
> 187....

LARGE WOMAN
Is anything wrong?

DANNY
Shut the fuck up.

She's startled but not intimidated, is about to respond, when Danny simply turns and walks out of the building.

EXT. AHAVAT TORAH—EVENING

He stops beneath an open window through which he hears...

RABBI'S AMPLIFIED VOICE
...Grant us peace, thy most precious gift, O Thou Eternal source of peace. We recall with loving memory those whom Thou hast summoned unto thee.

RABBI'S AMPLIFIED VOICE
And we mention by name...Sophie Budnitz...Bernard Schwabb...Milton Lifter... Aaron Lustig...Minnie Baum...

Danny closes his eyes, but at the end adds, under his breath:

DANNY
...Harriet Kantor Balint...

A half dozen VOICES, including Danny's, recite in unison...

DANNY & OTHERS
Yis-ga-dal v'yis-ka-dash sh'may ra-bo...

The body of the congregation joins in on certain phrases, producing a subtle and solemn music. Danny chants the entire prayer, and the moment it ends, and the rabbi begins the benediction....

> RABBI'S VOICE (AMPLIFIED)
> May the Lord bless you and keep you....

EXT. AHAVAT TORAH / STREET—EVENING

...he starts toward his car. But the Rabbi's VOICE seems to follow him, unnaturally loud and clear:

> RABBI (O.S.)
> May He cause the light of His countenance to shine upon you and be gracious unto you....

> DANNY
> (to himself)
> Eat shit....

> RABBI (O.S.)
> ...May you be blessed in your going forth as you were in your coming....

> DANNY
> (shouting to the empty street)
> EAT SHIT, ASSHOLES....

> RABBI (O.S.)
> And let us say...

> RABBI & CONGREGATION
> (with organ, singsong)
> Ah—ah—ah....men....

As Danny reaches the van, he sees the LARGE WOMAN silhouetted in the open doorway....

                    LARGE WOMAN
          YOU EAT SHIT.

Danny realizes he's still wearing the kippah. He throws it at her, but it only goes a couple of feet. He catches it, throws harder. This time it floats back toward him, and he has to jump out the way to keep it from hitting him. He gets in the car and drives off.

A WRISTWATCH: 12:05. We are:

EXT. FARMHOUSE—NIGHT

Danny hoists himself onto the kitchen roof. Above him is an open window, candlelight flickering. He starts into the room, stops....

INT. BEDROOM—NIGHT

Carla sits on the bed, straddling Curtis, who lies beneath her. She is looking right at Danny. Curtis, unaware of him, keeps thrusting into her from below.

Danny starts to leave, but on second thought stays. Carla stares expressionless, yet more attentive to him than to Curtis. Indeed, their eyes never leave each other, so that when she becomes aroused, we understand that it is Danny she is responding to, Danny she is really making love to.

Gradually her face loses its aloofness and seems to reach out to him, to reveal feelings that she can no longer deny. She holds her gaze until, at the final instant, she shudders out a series of stifled cries.

When she looks again, the window is empty.

INT. DANNY'S MOTEL ROOM—DAY

Danny reading. A KNOCK on the door. He looks up, Curtis comes in. Danny stiffens at the sight of him, but Curtis is friendly.

> CURTIS
>
> What are you reading?

Danny tilts the book to show him: *History of Political Philosophy.*

> CURTIS
>
> Leo Strauss...
> (nods approvingly)
> I've got to go to Boston. I came to say good-bye.

> DANNY
>
> What about Mrs. Moebius and...?

> CURTIS
>
> They left an hour ago.
> (off Danny's disappointment)
> You mind some personal advice? Forget Carla.
> That's not the side your bread's buttered on.
> (off Danny's silence)
> How soon can you get back to the city?

> DANNY
>
> A week or so. There's something I want to do here first.

> CURTIS
>
> What's that?

> (off Danny's silence)
> Okay. Surprise us...

INT. DARKNESS—NIGHT

The sound of SPLITTING WOOD. Then VOICES in a cavernous space...

> CHAOS OF VOICES
> Ow, shit...You're stepping on my fucking—
> ...Get off me...Goddammit...
>> (sounds of PUNCHES, a SCUFFLE)
> Stop it!...Where's the light?

One appears, illuminating nothing, dissipating into the still vaster darkness. A SERIES OF LIGHTS bang on in ecclesiastical bursts, illuminating: a vaulted ceiling...stained glass panels....We are:

INT. SYNAGOGUE SANCTUARY—NIGHT

A dour, ornate place built in the early decades of the century. The sight of it silences everyone for a moment. Then...

> CARLETON
> Jew World...!!

Drake, Billings, Carleton, O.L. and Steroid run wild...kicking over benches...spray-painting swastikas...hurling prayer books... urinating from the balcony....

...Danny looks around like someone revisiting his childhood home: slides his hand along a pew back...leafs through a chumash...gazes up at the eternal lamp behind its red glass...the gilded doors of the ark... A hint of Kol Nidre MUSIC haunts him....

> DANNY
> (to himself, barely a whisper)
> Shut up. Fuck you....

> KYLE (O.S.)
> What...?

Danny turns; Kyle is right behind him.

> DANNY
> Nothing. Where is it?
> (as Kyle hoists a sports bag)
> Okay, let's take one of these panels off so we
> can get under the bema...the stage.

As they unscrew a panel, Carleton runs past. A football flashes overhead. We hear GLASS BREAK...LAUGHTER.

INT. UNDER THE STAGE—NIGHT

DANNY WATCHES KYLE attach a bomb (four sticks of dynamite wired to a digital timer) to a 2x4 with a bungee cord. He hooks the ends, cautiously lets go. The cord springs free. The bomb falls.

Kyle gasps. Danny catches it.

Frozen, they look at each other. Kyle exhales, takes the bomb and, with Danny holding it, carefully restrings the bungee. A MECHANICAL NOISE overhead:

> STEROID (O.S.)
> Wow, look at this shit....

> DANNY
> What are they doing?

Kyle has no idea and doesn't care. Danny scrambles out.

INT. SANCTUARY—NIGHT

Straightening up, Danny is stunned by a vision:

THE OPEN ARK—THE TORAHS

...their silver crowns and breastplates, velvet robes. And Steroid Excess, lifting one out. Danny reacts with an instinctive horror.

>   DANNY
>   What are you doing? Put that down!
>   ...Put it back in there.

Steroid—cowed by Danny—starts to obey, but before he can...

>   BILLINGS
>   What do you care?

>   DANNY
>   I don't, but...

>   BILLINGS
>   (vaults onto the stage)
>   Let's look at the fucking thing.

Each CURSE makes Danny wince, but he just hovers about nervously as Billings and Steroid try to unwrap the Torah while others gather, some comically wrapping themselves in tallises.

>   DANNY
>   Put it there, on the...

He indicates the bema, stepping back as if to deny any involvement, yet at the same time trying to monitor everything they do.

> DANNY
> (indicating crowns, the yod...)

Just be careful with the...

> O.L.
> (puts a crown on his head)
> "If I were King of the forest...not Prince, not
> Duke, not Earl..."

Danny cannot endure this desecration, but everyone else laughs, so he keeps his mouth shut.

> KYLE

Open it up.

> DANNY
> (impulsively taking over)

Here...

He shoves his way in and, gripping the handles, unrolls the Torah. Low MURMURS at the sight of the broad columns, the mysterious calligraphy, the CRACKLING parchment. Danny himself is struck by the sudden immediacy of the sacred text. OVER this...

> VOICES

Oooo...Weird...You read it from right to left....The letters look like squashed bugs....What kind of paper is that?

> DANNY

It's not paper, it's parchment. It's made from sheepskin. And all the letters are drawn by hand.

                    KYLE
     Neat calligraphy.

Danny nods, then, as if against his will....

                    DANNY
     It's called the flame alphabet. It's supposed to
     be the word of God written in fire.

                    BILLINGS
     Fire...

                    DANNY
     The mystics tried to read the white spaces
     around the letters. They thought there was a
     whole alternative language hidden there, with
     secret, alternative meanings.

                    KYLE
     Cool.

Danny sees Drake watching him, smirks to express his disgust.

                    BILLINGS
     How come you know all this shit?

                    DANNY
     How come you don't know it?
                    (pressing the advantage)
     How can you say you hate the Jews when you
     don't know anything about—

                    BILLINGS
     Fuck you. I hate the Jews at least as much as
     you do.

                          DANNY
        No, you don't....If you hated them, you'd study
        them, so you'd know why you hate them. You
        know what tefillin is? Tsitsis? Shotness? You
        know the kaddish from the kiddush?
                          (obviously not)
        Eichmann? He went to Israel. He studied the
        Torah, the Talmud, the Mishnah, the whole
        bit. He hated Jews.

                        CARLETON
        Who's Eichmann?

                          DANNY
        Who's Eichmann?!!?

Danny's incredulous, though it's not clear how many of the others
know who Eichmann was.

                          KYLE
        He was head of the Gestapo's Jewish sector.
        He deported people to the camps.

                        CARLETON
                (reaching toward he parchment)
        Can we touch it?

                          DANNY
        Yeah, but not on the letters.

                         BILLINGS
        Why the fuck not?

                          DANNY
                  (warning finger)
        Just don't.

Billings bristles at Danny's authority; Carleton says to him...

> CARLETON
>
> Didn't you see *Raiders of the Lost Ark*?

> BILLINGS
>
> What??

> CARLETON
>
> That was an ark, man. That was a Torah. They
> fucked around with it, and the Torah melted
> their faces.

> BILLINGS
>
> That's a movie, you moron.

> CARLETON
>
> Fine, go ahead. Touch the letters.

The others are gathered around, delicately touching the sheepskin.

> BILLINGS
>
> Let me see.

He pushes through, looks at the Torah. He runs his fingers over
the crinkled parchment, the smooth black letters.

> DANNY
>
> I said not on the—

Suddenly Billings grabs the parchment in both hands and tries to
tear it. It's tougher than it looks.

> DANNY
>
> Stop it! What are you doing?

He tries to stop him, but—accidentally or not—Drake gets in the way, and before Danny can do anything else, Billings crumples it and finally tears a long gash into the scroll.

This produces a strange effect on the others. Some (Kyle, Steroid, Drake) join in. They knock the aitz off the bema, it rolls out, exposing ten feet of Torah. They stamp on it, spit on it.... Others (Carleton, O.L.), though less troubled than Danny, are surprised (and embarrassed) by their own revulsion at these acts.

Danny watches helplessly, like the survivor who did nothing as his son was murdered.

Finally the Torah lies torn and soiled on the stage. A strange silence.

                    KYLE
          Let's get out of here.

...Danny kneels by the Torah. With a tallis, he attempts to clean the parchment. Carleton and O.L. help him roll it onto the aitz. [Echo "Christ taken down from cross" with Torah as Christ.] They replace the cover, the yod, the crowns....

Finally Danny lifts it up, holds it to him as if it were his dead child. He closes his eyes, murmurs to himself....

                    DANNY
          Shema yisrael adonai elohenu adonai echod.

                    CARLETON
          What'd you say?

                    DANNY
          Nothing. Let's go....

He starts to walk out, carrying the Torah.

                    CARLETON
        Why are you taking that?

                    DANNY
        I'm stealing it.

EXT. AHAVAT TORAH—DAY

A VIDEO IMAGE:

                    NEWSCASTER VOICE (V.O.)
        ...Tragedy was barely averted today at Temple
        Ahavat Torah when a bomb planted under the
        bema failed to detonate....

                    KYLE (O.S.)
        Shit!

                    NEWSCASTER VOICE (V.O.)
        ...Authorities say that if it had, injuries and
        loss of life could have been in the dozens....

INT. DANNY'S MOTEL ROOM—DAY

Danny, Kyle and others watching the TV.

                    NEWSCASTER VOICE
        Channel 8's Cindy Pomerantz spoke to Rabbi
        Malcolm Weiss.

ON TV: Cindy (sleek, sexy) and the rabbi (handsome, vain).

                    CINDY (ON TV)
        Rabbi, how is it that disaster and tragedy were
        averted here today at Ahavat Torah?

RABBI (ON TV)
Apparently the power cell in the timer gave
out precisely thirteen minutes before the
device was set to go off.

RABBI (ON TV)
So we can only conclude that once again God
has intervened to save the Jewish people....

DANNY
(giving the finger to the TV)
Oh, fuck you...

RABBI (ON TV)
As you know, Cindy, thirteen is a mystical
number in the Jewish faith. We believe that
God has thirteen attributes...

Danny is beside himself.

RABBI (ON TV)
...Of which the highest is ein sof, which means
"without end," or, sometimes, "nothingness
without end...."

CINDY (ON TV)
Nothingness without end...That's very interesting.

RABBI (ON TV)
The purest form of spirit...

ON DANNY. Sound fades. He's haunted: "Nothingness without
end" was what he'd told Guy Daniels the Jews were obsessed with.
He seems to hear the cello playing "Kol Nidre" again. Then...

DANNY

Okay, everybody out. Get out.

He switches off the TV. Shoves them out the door, slams it.

INT. DANNY'S MOTEL ROOM—LATER

Alone he sits at the desk, finds himself gazing at the Torah, standing in a corner of his closet, draped in the tallis.

He slams the closet door, it bounces open. Slams it again, making sure it latches.

He sits down, looks at the closed door until, in bitter resignation he gets up and opens it again.

He unrolls the Torah on the bed...Scotch tapes the tear closed... attempts to clean the stain with a moistened cloth.

INT. DANNY'S MOTEL ROOM—DAY

Danny is in the bathroom in front of the mirror, holding his shirt up with his chin as he wraps the tallis around his torso. When he lowers the shirt, the fringes hang out like the tsitsis that Orthodox men wear.

He feels a weird loathing for this, but he smooths and arranges the tsitsis to look just like a Hasid's. He clicks his heels together and gives a Nazi salute.

DANNY

Alenu l'shab'ach la'adon hacol...

Another Nazi salute. A KNOCK at the door. He hides the fringes under the shirt, throws a blanket over the Torah.

DANNY

What?

STEROID (O.S.)

Phone, Danny.

EXT. MOTEL—PAY PHONE—DAY

GUY'S VOICE (PHONE)

Danny Balint...Guy Danielsen, *New York Times*.

DANNY
(tucks in the tallis fringes)

What do you want? What happened to your
article?

GUY'S VOICE (PHONE)

I couldn't get my editor to run it, but I bet he
will now that you've put a bomb in a synagogue. That was you, wasn't it, Danny?

Danny hangs up. Stands there. A VOICE makes him jump....

VOICE (DRAKE)

Hey, Danny, want to kill a Jew?

Danny turns: it's Drake. These are the first words he's spoken.

EXT. SUBURBAN STREET/INT. CAR—DAY

Danny and Drake pass a low-slung modern synagogue. A sign
announces: AMBASSADOR ILIO MANZETTI Friday, August
31. Danny reacts, startled...Drake smiles.

DRAKE

Park up there, we'll walk back.

EXT. CONGREGATION BETH SHALOM—TWILIGHT

The building is lit. Within we hear an AMPLIFIED VOICE, presumably Manzetti giving a speech. We can't make out the words.
Danny and Drake are hidden among the rhododendrons flanking
the parking lot. Danny is watching a door in the side of the
building and eating a sandwich as Drake loads a scoped rifle.

> DRAKE
> Lie on your stomach and come up on your
> elbows.

> DANNY
> Why me?

> DRAKE
> You want to kill a Jew. I already did.

Danny assumes the prone position, Drake sets the rifle in his hands.

> DANNY
> Who'd you kill?

> DRAKE
> Four. But no one this important.

We hear APPLAUSE within as the speech ends.

> DRAKE
> Okay, it's over. He'll take a couple questions,
> then come out....Sight down the rifle toward
> the door.

THROUGH RIFLE SCOPE: Danny pans from the side door—
where TWO MEN are smoking—to a waiting limousine.

> DANNY
> How did you know they were Jews?

                    DRAKE
        I can tell....

                    DANNY
    How?

                    DRAKE
        I was a Jew in a previous life.

Before Danny can respond, Drake gestures toward the synagogue.

                    DRAKE
        Here they come.

Danny puts his eye back to the scope.

SCOPE POV: stirring at the door. The men put out their ciga-
rettes. Three figures emerge: a MAN and a WOMAN on either
side of an older, distinguished-looking man (MANZETTI). They
walk this way.

                    DRAKE (O.S.)
        Shoot him in the head. Always shoot a Jew in
        the head.

                    DANNY
        I'm a bad shot. I don't think I can—

                    DRAKE (O.S.)
        Just get him in the cross-hairs. With those
        shells, anywhere you hit him, it'll bounce
        around, rip his insides all up.

SCOPE POV: the TRIO walking this way, cross-hairs on
Manzetti.

>   DRAKE (O.S.)
>   Right there! Just squeeze the trigger.
>   Slow...Do it!

Danny FIRES, misses. Everybody hits the ground.

>   DRAKE
>   You missed on purpose.

>   DANNY
>   I didn't. I told you, I can't—

>   DRAKE
>   What's that?

Danny looks over his shoulder. His shirt has ridden up his back, revealing the tallis wrapped around his waist.

>   DRAKE
>   I knew it.

Drake pulls a .45 from the duffel....Without thinking, Danny rolls over, fires the rifle. Drake is blown backward, dropping the .45.

Danny leaps up....Drake's on his hands and knees, his trousers quickly darkening with blood. Danny's upset.

>   DANNY
>   Oh, Jesus...Drake, are you okay...?

FOOTSTEPS, coming this way. Danny runs. We hear voices, "Get down....Stay down....He's got a gun...." Drake picks himself up, stumbles away, bent over....

EXT. QUEENS—DUSK
Danny parks the van in an abandoned lot near the river. Quickly

wiping down the wheel with his shirt, he tosses out his duffel bag and the scoped rifle. He climbs out, wipes down the door, throws the rifle into the water, grabs the duffel and hurries away.

> DANNY (V.O.)
> Kyle, it's me Danny. How you doing?... I had to
> come into the city to see Mrs. MOEBIUS....No,
> I gave Drake the van, didn't he bring it back?

INT. DANNY'S APARTMENT—NIGHT

Danny's on the phone, whipping through several newspapers.

> DANNY
> ...Since when?... Really? And he didn't call?...
> No, I don't know...

He finds a tiny item: "Gunfire Reported at Synagogue." He scans it: no mention of Drake or himself.

> DANNY
> Sure, come on down....Can you bring my
> stuff?...Thanks...and if Drake shows up, let me
> know right away....Good...

He hangs up. From behind some books, he extracts the small-caliber handgun he found in his father's house earlier.

INT. MRS. MOEBIUS'S APARTMENT — TWILIGHT

Danny alone, waiting, nervous. He hears FOOTSTEPS approach, he touches the gun in the back of his trousers.
Lina and Curtis enter.

> LINA
> How have things been going?

DANNY
(how much do they know?)
Fine.

LINA
(indicates a chair)
We want to talk to you about something....
(as they sit, Danny nervous)
We're about to launch an aboveground, intellectually serious fascist movement.

Danny's is relieved and intrigued. Lina nods at Curtis to go on.

CURTIS
We want to build bridges to certain positions
in the political mainstream: works like *The
Bell Curve, Sociobiology,* anti-Zionism, anti-
immigration, the com-munitarian issue....
We'll hold conferences: invite liberals, blacks,
Jews. Chomsky, Cockburn, Stanley Crouch,
Shahack....

DANNY
I've been waiting all my life for something like
this.

MRS. MOEBIUS
We want you to help run it. Give speeches,
lead seminars... Handle the fund-raising.

DANNY
(slapped in the face)
Fund-raising??

MRS. MOEBIUS
We think you'd be good at it.

OFF-SCREEN we hear the front door. FEET come up the stairs....

> DANNY
> What about...Manzetti, the synagogues....

> CURTIS
> That doesn't seem to be happening, does it?

> DANNY
> I've been stuck out in the country with those
> guys who just want to paint swastikas and heil
> Hitler. How am I supposed to—(get anything
> done there?)

He stops short as Carla walks into the room from shopping. She glances at them, puts down her bags, goes into the kitchen....

> CURTIS
> Danny, the night we met, you said the name Ilio
> Manzetti. We were impressed. We were excited.
> But here it is September, and Mr. Manzetti is
> still walking around breathing the air.

> MRS. MOEBIUS
> We need intellectuals, we have enough thugs
> already.

Danny's watching Carla go down the hall toward the back, can barely bring his attention back to the conversation at hand.

> DANNY
> I'm not an intellectual.... I mean, I read,
> but...Fund-raising isn't what I...

> MRS. MOEBIUS
> Look, if you want to kill Jews on your free

time, fine. We need you to raise money. Will
you do that for us?

He nods but cannot look at her.

> MRS. MOEBIUS
> Thank you.

He's dismissed. He rises.

> MRS. MOEBIUS
> Do you have a suit?
> > (off Danny; to Curtis)
> Let's get him one....And a cell phone too.
> > (as Danny turns to go; a joke for her own amusement)
> And if you insist on blowing up a synagogue,
> make it that big one on Fifth Avenue, would you?

> DANNY
> Beth Shalom? It's Reform.

> MRS. MOEBIUS
> So what?

> DANNY
> They're not that Jewish.

> MRS. MOEBIUS
> I don't care what they are. I know those
> people, and I don't like them. The rest are just
> a bunch of kikes, aren't the?

She smiles. He manages a smile back and hurries away, face
burning with shame.

EXT. MOEBIUS APARTMENT, STREET—NIGHT

Danny comes out of the building, squats between two parked cars and vomits, retching spastically until, gasping for breath...

> VOICE
>
> Here...

He turns. Carla walks over to him, wipes his mouth with a crumpled tissue. When she moves to kiss him, he holds back, shy about the smell, but she kisses him anyway, on the mouth.

INT. DANNY'S APARTMENT—NIGHT

Carla, naked, browsing the books, sees something in the closet. It's the Torah Danny took from the synagogue. She unrolls it on the bed, her gaze moving over the mysterious, glossy script. Danny, coming out of the bathroom, sees what she is doing, and stops short.

> CARLA
>
> Where'd you get this?

> DANNY
>
> I stole it. From a synagogue.

She looks at the broad printed columns....

> CARLA
>
> How come there's no punctuation?

> DANNY
>
> That was a later invention, it's not in the scrolls....Anyway, the Jews know where the sentences end. They know the whole thing by heart. Every word. Every letter.

> CARLA
>
> Do you know it like that? By heart.

                    DANNY
No.

                    CARLA
But you can read it, the Hebrew....Right?

                    DANNY
What do you care?

                    CARLA
'Cause I want to know....What is this word?
This one here...

Danny looks at the word, then back at her. He's torn between
competing desires, but finally...

                    DANNY
Va-yomer...And he said.
         (she moves her finger to the left)
It goes the other way.

                    CARLA
         (she knew that)
Oh, yeah...
         (moves finger right)

                    DANNY
Va-yomer adonai el Avram: lech lecha may-
artzcha oo-mimohlad-tcha oo-m'bayt avaycha
el ha-ertez asher arecha...

                    CARLA
What's it mean?

                    DANNY
And God said to Avram, take yourself away

from your land and from the place you were
born and from your father's house into the
land—a different land—that I will show you....

Danny remains silent a moment, affected by the passage....

                    CARLA
I want to learn to read it.

                    DANNY
Why?

                    CARLA
Know your enemy....'Cause it's a basic text of
Western culture. I want to read it in the orig-
inal. Okay?

                    DANNY
Hebrew's very difficult. It would take years.

                    CARLA
I'm good at languages.

He looks at the smooth expanse of her back, the articulations of
her spine. He finds her very beautiful.

                    DANNY
Put something on. You're not supposed to be
naked in front of it.
                    CARLA
Why not?

                    DANNY
They think it's the word of God, and it's holy,
and the flesh isn't....

CARLA

That's stupid.

DANNY

Yeah, it's stupid.
            (indicating her T-shirt)
Put it on, or I won't teach you.

She grudgingly pulls on the shirt as he gets a pencil and paper.

DANNY

See, the Jews love to separate things: the holy
from the profane, milk from meat, wool from
linen, the Sabbath from the week, the Jew
from the gentile....As if one little scrap of this
was going to completely contaminate that.

CARLA

What assholes.

DANNY

You can't curse in front of it either.

He shrugs as if indifferent to these rules, yet compelled to point
them out.

CARLA

Who gets contaminated, the Jews or the
gentiles?

DANNY

Good question. Both.
            (draws a letter)
Aleph...

CARLA

It looks a little like a swastika.

DANNY

It's silent. It holds a place, takes a vowel. The vowels are little dots that go under the letters.

CARLA

Where are they?

DANNY

They don't put them in the Torah. I'll get you a chumash, they'll have them there...Bet...Gimel...Dalid...Hay...
(as she repeats the names)
How come you're here instead of with Curtis? Besides the Hebrew lessons...

CARLA

The sex is better.

DANNY

Even though his dick is so big?

CARLA

With you there's a tragic dimension.

DANNY

Vuv...Zayin...Chet...Tet...

He writes each letter as he says it, and she repeats after him.

EXT. WILLIAMSBURG BRIDGE—DAY

Danny and Kyle.

                    KYLE
This will be a different kind of device.

                    DANNY
That damn thing. You know how it made me
look...?

                    KYLE
I'm sorry, Danny. It won't happen again. I'm
going to use a brand-new power cell. Plus we'll
have a back-up timer.

                    DANNY
I've gotta kill some Jews, Kyle. I'm serious.
I'm always talking about it. This time it's
gotta happen.

                    KYLE
It will.

Kyle's confident, and the prospect of this really happening gives
Danny pause. He feels a brief chill, escapes it with...

                    DANNY
What about Drake, did he ever show up?

                    KYLE
No, it's weird, man. Nobody knows where he
went.

Danny nods, gestures for Kyle to split. Kyle looks around, walks
away. Danny waits a moment, then heads in the opposite direction.

EXT. WILLIAMSBURG—DAY

Danny walking behind a Hasidic family (MAN, WOMAN, 3-year-old BOY, STROLLER)...watching them. At a corner, the father takes the boy's hand, and as they cross the street, the boy glances back at Danny.

EXT. COUNTRY ROAD—DAY, 1943

TWO NAZI SOLDIERS have just discovered a JEWISH FAMILY hiding in the back of a hay wagon. The POLISH MAN is holding the little boy.

As a soldier tries to take the BOY out of his arms, the child panics, clings to his father, screaming, "Papa...Papa..." It is the scene the survivor described in the meeting with the Nazis. But now the father is DANNY'S FATHER....

> FATHER (IN POLISH)
> ...Hush, come on, don't cry. Everything will be
> all right....

A Nazi sergeant comes over, irritated. *The sergeant is Danny.*

> DANNY/NAZI SERGEANT
> (in German)
> What's the matter here?

> FATHER
> (to the sergeant, in German)
> Excuse me, I'm sorry, just a moment...

The sergeant rips the child out of his arms. The kid becomes hysterical. The father manages to take the boy's hand.

> FATHER
> (in Polish)
> Please, sweetheart, you have to go. I'll see you soon.

In an access of disgust, the sergeant sticks his bayonet into the boy—or rather, into something offscreen. We hear a terrible sound, the child grunts. The family gasps in horror.

Danny/sergeant lifts the (unseen) child into the air. Its SHADOW darkens the father's face. Drops of blood run down his cheeks....

Danny/sergeant stares into the father's face, enraged at the man's passivity.

> DANNY/NAZI SERGEANT
> Fucking kike.

EXT. STREET—DAY

DANNY'S FACE—sweating, haunted, as if he's just woken from the previous.

He's still walking down the street, but now, as if to flee his thoughts, he steps through a door into...

INT. BOOKSTORE—DAY

A Jewish bookstore. He grabs the first book that comes to hand, reads for a moment, throws it down in disgust. Picks it up again, is still reading when...

> VOICE
> Hey, Danny...Danny...

He looks up at a young man about his own age; wearing a yarmulke, but otherwise normal, hair clean, beard neatly trimmed.

> YOUNG MAN
> It's Stuart. Stuart Schoenbaum.

                    DANNY
Shlomo?

                    STUART
Yeah...

Danny puts down the book, trying to conceal that he's been
reading it. He offers a hand. Stuart manages to restrain the
impulse to embrace him, but takes the hand warmly.

                    STUART
Jeez, it's been since, what, Kenny's wedding.

                    DANNY
Yeah, uh... So how are you? What's going on?

                    STUART
I'm in the rabbinic program at JTS...

                    DANNY
JTS...?

                    STUART
What about you? What are you doing? Something strange, I bet.

                    DANNY
I'm in a kind of...underground...thing.

                    STUART
                (impressed, excited)
Are you an artist?

                    DANNY
No, no... Not that kind of...underground.
More a private...business. Private.

Meaning he can't talk about it. Stuart nods. Danny notices a young woman: dark, curly hair, sharp eyes.

> STUART
> You remember Miriam....

> DANNY
> Yeah, hey, how're you doing...

> MIRIAM
> Hey...

An irony to her. They certainly remember each other.

> STUART
> She's at Yale Law now—interning with the
> district attorney....
> (Miriam makes a face)
> We're getting married next spring. In Israel.

> DANNY
> Wow, that's uh...great...

He glances at Miriam; but she has picked up the book he'd been reading, is leafing through it. It makes him uneasy.

> STUART
> It's great seeing you....

> MIRIAM
> Maybe Danny'd like to come to the minyan
> for the holidays....

Danny gives her a dirty look, but Stuart's thrilled:

                    STUART

Oh, good idea. We're davening with this
group from the seminary. Interesting people,
very open-minded, you might like them. And
guess who comes...Avi! You guys could go at it
again like the old days.

As Stuart scribbles an address...

                    STUART

Danny and Avi used to argue about everything: Torah, Talmud, politics, girls. It always
ended in a fistfight.

                    MIRIAM

I remember.

                    DANNY

I always won.

                    MIRIAM

The arguments, anyway.

                    STUART
            (hands Danny the address)
It's at K.I. on 101st. In the little chapel. Try to
make it. It'd be fun.

Danny smiles. He has no intention of going. Once they leave, he
picks up the book and resumes reading.

INT. AN EXECUTIVE SUITE —DAY

ROGER BRAND, a high-powered CEO, sits behind a big desk,
speed-reading something through half-glasses. He finishes,
removes the glasses. A *New York Times* is on the desk.

                    BRAND
You write that?
                    (as Danny nods)
Come work for me. You've got a lot to learn; I
can teach it to you.

                    DANNY
I have a job.

                    BRAND
This? This is a joke.
                    (tossing down the pages)
I'll give your group a thousand bucks.

                    DANNY
You gave fifty thousand to that college magazine.

                    BRAND
Fifty's an exaggeration. Anyway, that was a different moment. Things were possible then
that aren't now.

                    DANNY
Actually, I think this moment has possibilities
that—

                    BRAND
Yeah, I read your piece. It's very smart. And
very wrong.

Brand's phone beeps, he touches a button, continues.

                    BRAND
Forget the Jewish stuff. It doesn't play anymore.

> (over Danny's)
> There's only the market, now, and it doesn't
> care who you are.

                    DANNY
People still need values, beliefs....

                    BRAND
No, they don't. Not the smart ones.
          (because he likes him)
Look, I'll give you five grand if you can document your tax-exempt status....But when you
fall off this horse, come see me. I can show
you how to make a lot of money.

                    DANNY
I don't care about money.

                    BRAND
You will.

                    DANNY
You're a Jew. You don't realize it, but you are.

                    BRAND
          (smiles, uninsulted)
Maybe I am. Maybe we're all Jews now.
What's the difference?

On Danny, troubled by this.

INT. A SMALL LECTURE HALL—EVENING

A half-dozen white lumpen sit at desks. Danny writes "ANTI-
SEMITISM" in large letters on a blackboard. He turns....

DANNY

How many of you think of yourselves as anti-
Semites?

(All the hands go up.)

Good. Actually, the term is a bit imprecise
since technically Jews are only one of the
Semitic peoples.... In fact, Arabs are Semites,
as are the Eritreans, the Ethiopians and so
on.... But for our purposes an anti-Semite is
someone who hates or is against Jews.... Now,
why do we hate them?

He looks around. The room is silent.

DANNY

Let me put it another way. Do we hate them
because they push their way in where they
don't belong? Or because they're clannish and
keep to themselves?

Murmurs of "Yeah. Both." But some are confused by this.

INT. SAME—ANOTHER DAY

Slightly bigger crowd, a few middle-class-looking people.

DANNY

...Because they're tight with money, or because
they flash it around? Because they're Bolshe-
viks or because they're capitalists? Because
they have the highest IQs, or because they
have the most active sex lives?

The audience, confused...

                    DANNY
      Do you want to know the real reason we hate
      them?...

INT. SAME—DAY

...More people: white collar workers of both sexes, nurses, artists.
Lapel buttons, bumper stickers backpacks: "FIGHT NEW
WORLD DISORDER" "STOP THE WTO" "EARTH FIRST!"

                    DANNY
      ...Because we hate them.
              (as people exchange puzzled looks)
      Because they exist. Because it is an axiom of
      civilization that just as man longs for woman,
      loves his children and fears death, he hates
      the Jews.

                    DANNY
              (smiles)
      There is no reason. If there were, some smart-
      ass kike would give us an argument, try to
      prove we were wrong. And of course that
      would only make us hate them more. In fact
      we have all the reasons we need in three
      simple letters: J-E-W. Jew. Say it a million
      times. It is the only word that never loses its
      meaning: Jew Jew Jew Jew Jew Jew Jew Jew
      Jew Jew Jew Jew Jew....

EXT. NEW JERSEY MEADOWLANDS—DAWN

Danny and Kyle sitting in the tall grass looking across the marsh-
lands toward the Manhattan skyline shimmering in the distance.

> KYLE
> (sings, looking at watch)
> "My country 'tis of thee, Sweet land of liberty,
> Of thee I..."

He points sharply and an explosion occurs thirty yards away. They run over, pick up the mangled timer. They're pleased.

EXT. JCC (ANSCHE CHESED)—DAY

A couple of stragglers hurry through the main doors as we hear...

> VOICES
> B'Rosh Hashanah yika-teyvun, uv'yom tsom
> kippur yey-chateymun..

INT. SMALL CHAPEL—DAY

Rosh Hashanah services. A woman is davening....

> WOMAN
> And it came to pass after these things that
> God tested Abraham...

DANNY... sitting with Stuart and Miriam...

> WOMAN (O.S.)
> ...And said to him, "Abraham." And he said,
> "Here am I..." And God said, "Take your son,
> your only son, whom you love..."

> DANNY
> (to himself)
> It's not his only son....

ANOTHER VOICE
The only one he loves.

Danny looks at AVI (athletic, smooth-shaven) who grins sardon-
ically and fakes a punch as...

DANNY
They only kill them when they love them?

AVI
(sliding into a seat next to them)
What are you doing here, I thought you were
a Nazi.

STUART
Come on, Avi...

AVI
You know what this guy told me once: Islam
and Judaism both start with Abraham mur-
dering his son: first sending Ishmael into the
desert, then sacrificing Isaac....

VOICES
Shhhh...Can you please be quiet?

DANNY
And Christianity's the same, with minor variations.

AVI
Ridiculous.
(to the people around them)
Folks, don't listen to this guy. He's a well-
known anti-Semite.

MIRIAM

Avi, please...

AVI
(snatching off Danny's hat)
...Look, he's a skinhead.

VOICES
It's just a style, Avi....There are antiracist
skins.

AVI
(laughing)
Believe me, Danny's the racist kind. Are you a
fascist, Danny? Yes or no.

DANNY
What's a fascist?

AVI
I rest my case. He's a Jewish Nazi. He always
was.

DANNY
Whereas Avi's an Zionist Nazi.

AVI
The Zionists aren't Nazis.

DANNY
They're racist, they're militaristic, they act
like bullyboys in the territories....

AVI
They don't have extermination camps.

DANNY
They had Sabra and Shattila.

MIRIAM
Do you hate them because they're wimps or
because they're bullyboys?

Danny's startled by the question, but before he can react...

AVI
(over her, to Danny)
That was the Lebanese, that wasn't—

VOICES (O.S.)
The Israeli Army knew about the camps.
Sharon encouraged the falangists to go in
there and murder all the—

AVI
You don't know that. There's no—

DANNY
Read the early Zionists on European Jewry;
they sound like Goebbels.

MIRIAM
They sound like you.

DANNY
The Nazis did everything the führer told
them. You do everything the Torah tells you.
Or the rebbe. Identical slave mentality.

Avi lunges at him. They begin pounding each other. Chaos.

EXT. STREET—NIGHT

Miriam and Danny walk down West End Avenue together. He's oddly relaxed with her?

> MIRIAM
> Why did you come tonight? To see me?

> DANNY
> (after a beat)
> To hear them read Torah.

> MIRIAM
> I thought you hated Torah.

> DANNY
> That doesn't mean I don't like hearing it.

> MIRIAM
> Point out all the lies and fucked-up thinking.

She smiles and even he smiles a little. They walk together, oddly companionable.

> MIRIAM
> You know the joke: a Jew's shipwrecked on a
> desert island. When they rescue him, they see
> he's built two synagogues. They say, For vhat
> you need two synagogues? He says, vun to
> pray in, and vun I'd never set foot in so long
> as I live, so help me God.
> (he nods, he's heard it)
> You pray in the one you'd never set foot
> in...and vice versa.

> DANNY
> I can't help what I think.

MIRIAM

This is me.

She stops in front of a nice doorman building. He's impressed.

MIRIAM

Tell me about Lina Moebius.

DANNY
(startled)

How did you...?

MIRIAM

I work in the DA's office. You go to those meetings, half the people there are inform-
ants.

DANNY

You mean the *Times* guy?

MIRIAM

Which *Times* guy?

DANNY

With the shoes...There was more than one?

In an excess of paranoia, he walks away. She calls after him....

MIRIAM

Danny...Danny...
(he doesn't look back)
Shit...

INT. DANNY'S APARTMENT — NIGHT

Sweltering heat. A fan ruffles Carla's hair as she lies on the futon going back and forth between Hebrew/English Torah and a Hebrew grammar. Danny is on the floor lifting weights.

> CARLA
> (slowly, laboriously)
> Payn tash-chiton v'ashiytem...

> DANNY
> (correcting her)
> V'asitem...

> CARLA
> V'asitem lechem pessel to-monat. And make no graven image of the Lord, or the form of any figure, or of man or woman, or beast or fowl or fish or anything that looks like anything. Because He's not like anything. Not only can't you see Him or hear Him, you can't even think about Him. I mean, what's the difference between that and Him not existing?

> DANNY
> (still exercising)
> No difference.

> CARLA
> Christianity's silly, but at least there's something to believe in. Or not believe. Judaism there's nothing.

> DANNY
> (to himself)
> Nothing but nothingness...Judaism's not about belief.

                    CARLA
What's it about?

                    DANNY
About doing things. You light candles, say
prayers, keep the Sabbath, visit the sick....

                    CARLA
And belief follows?

                    DANNY
No. Nothing follows. You don't do it because
it's smart or stupid or it saves your soul.
You're not saved. Nobody's saved. You do it
because the Torah tells you to. You submit to
the Torah.

                    CARLA
Fuck that.

                    DANNY
Don't curse in front of it.

                    CARLA
            (flips the book closed)
Why should I submit?

                    DANNY
You shouldn't.

                    CARLA
You think I should just because there's no
reason?

He looks at her without answering.

> DANNY
> No, I think you shouldn't.

> CARLA
> Judaism doesn't even need God. You have the
> Torah, the law. That's your fucking God....
> (anticipating his objections)
> The book's closed.

In an access of something, she bites his arm, hard. He winces, pushes her away. She kisses the place she bit. He starts to play with her hair....

> DANNY
> You're learning the Hebrew really fast.

> CARLA
> I told you, I'm good at this.

> DANNY
> Plus you have nothing else to do all day.

> CARLA
> Oh, am I learning it faster than you did?
> Maybe I'm smarter.

He laughs, he likes her arrogance. But she misunderstands:

> CARLA
> Is that funny? You think Jews are the only
> smart ones?

As they make out, grow aroused...

> DANNY
> What...? You think I'm Jewish?

It's all you talk about. Jewish, Jewish, Jewish.
Nobody talks about it that much except the
Jews.

Danny's taken aback by the simple logic.

DANNY
Nazis talk about it all the time.

CARLA
Do they?

And, of course, she has grown up among Nazis.

DANNY
The real Nazis. Hitler, Goebbels, they talked
about Jews incessantly.... You ever read their
diaries?...

CARLA
Is that why you became a Nazi? So you could
talk about Jews incessantly?

DANNY
Believe me, Adolf Hitler couldn't possibly
have hated the Jews as much as I do. Not in a
billion years. You know why?

CARLA
'Cause he wasn't a rabbi.

DANNY
You want a punch in the mouth?

CARLA

Okay...
(he doesn't hit her)
Why don't we light candles on Friday? Let's
light candles....And say the kaddish.

DANNY

Kaddish is the prayer for the dead.

CARLA

I mean kiddush. Let's say kiddush. And shave
my head, fuck through a sheet, all that stuff...
(as he walks away)
Come on, just for fun. To see what it's like...

INT. SMALL LECTURE HALL—NIGHT

Packed with a well-dressed crowd, very different from the crowds
we've seen here before.

DOWN IN FRONT: Mrs. Moebius and Danny talk in low tones.

MRS. MOEBIUS

Half the right-wing money in New York is
here tonight. They came to see you. If you
impress them, if you do what I know you can,
this movement will be up and running by
tomorrow. And on the front page of the *New
York Times* in six months.

She straightens his tie, directs him toward the lecturn. He
hesiates....

DANNY

We tested the new bomb.

MRS. MOEBIUS
What?

DANNY
We redesigned the timing mechanism. It can't
possibly malfunction.

MRS. MOEBIUS
Danny, please. Just give your speech....And
nothing about Jews, okay?

She walks away.

INT. SMALL LECTURE HALL—STAGE—NIGHT

Danny steps to the lectern. The CROWD QUIETS. He stands
silent for a long moment, then closes his eyes and chants with feeling:

DANNY
Shema yisroel adonai elohenu adonai echod.

General confusion. Mrs. Moebius and Curtis exchange wary glances.

DANNY
Who knows what that is?

VOICE
A Jewish prayer.

DANNY
Can anybody imagine why I would say a
Jewish prayer?

ANOTHER VOICE
Because you're a Jew.

Nervous laughter. Danny laughs with them.

> DANNY
> That could be one reason. What's another?
> (no response)
> Let me put it this way... who here would like
> to destroy the Jews?
> (murmurs of approval)
> Who wants to grind their bones into the dust?

A scattering of applause, growing more sustained...

> DANNY
> And who wants to see them rise again,
> wealthier, more successful, powerful, cultured
> and intelligent than ever?

Silence. No one wants that.

> DANNY
> Then you know what you have to do?...
> You have to love them.

Puzzled mutterings: "What?...What's he talking about?..."

> DANNY
> Did he say love them? Love the Jews? It
> sounds strange, I know, but with these people
> nothing is simple. The Jew says that all he
> wants is to be left alone to study his Torah, do
> a little business and fornicate with his over-
> sexed wife....But it isn't true. He wants to be
> hated. He longs for our scorn. He clings to it
> as if it were the very core and mystery of his
> being. If Hitler had not existed, the Jews
> would have invented him.

DANNY

For without such hatred, the so-called Chosen
People would vanish from the earth....

People react with confusion, uncertainty, suspicion.

DANNY

...And this reveals a terrible truth, the crux of
our problem as Nazis: the worse the Jews are
treated, the stronger they become. Egyptian
slavery made them a nation; the pogroms
hardened them; Auschwitz gave birth to the
State of Israel. Suffering, it seems, is the very
crucible of their genius.
If the Jews are, as one of their own has said, a
people who will not take yes for an answer,
then let us say yes to them. If they thrive on
opposition, let us cease to oppose them. The
way to annihilate them, utterly and completely, is to open our arms, take them into
our homes and embrace them. Only then will
they vanish into assimilation, dilution...and
love.
(a warning finger)
But we cannot pretend. The Jew is nothing if
not clever. He will see through condescension
and hypocrisy. To destroy him, we will have to
love him sincerely.

ON THE AUDIENCE, befuddled. A HAND goes up. Danny
nods to it. The man steps forward, and we see that it's Guy
Danielsen of the *Times*. Danny is shaken....

GUY

But if the Jews are strengthened by hate,
wouldn't this "destruction" you speak of—by

love or any other means—in fact make them
more powerful than they are already?

> DANNY
> (after a beat)
> Yes. Infinitely more. They would become as
> God.

Murmurs of confusion, outrage..."God???!!!" Danny notices the
TALLIS crawling out from under his shirt, stuffs it back in.

> DANNY
> It is the Jews' destiny to be annihilated so that
> they can be deified....

> DANNY
> (the murmurs swell)
> Jesus understood this perfectly. And look what
> was accomplished there with the death of just
> one enlightened Jew. Imagine what would
> happen if we killed them all!!
> (over the rising outrage)
> So, let us say together...Shema yisroel...

One or two voices respond, but most people shout him down.
Mrs. Moebius is outraged. People are throwing things, shouting.
The meeting degenerates into chaos.

INT. MOEBIUS APARTMENT—DAY

Danny talks to Mrs. Moebius. Offscreen we hear a TV.

> MRS. MOEBIUS
> Are you out of your mind?!

DANNY
I was just trying to make a point. If—

CARLA (O.S.)
Oh, my God...
                    (calling)
Lina...

MRS. MOEBIUS
I'm relieving you of all duties. I don't want
you working for us anymore....

DANNY
You can't. Do you know how many people I've
brought into...the movement...?

CURTIS (O.S.)
Lina, come here!

INT. KITCHEN—DAY

Carla watching a small TV on the kitchen counter. Danny arrives,
followed by Linda and Curtis as we hear...

REPORTER (O.S.)
According to police, he had just left the
restaurant and was walking the block and a
half back to his office, when the gunman
stepped out of this doorway, fired seven times
at point-blank range...then fled on foot.

DANNY
            (a terrible premonition)
Who was it?

Mrs. Moebius impatiently signals him to silence.

                    REPORTER (O.S.)
          ...Paramedics arrived within ninety seconds,
          but Mr. Manzetti was declared dead at the
          scene.

At the mention of Manzetti's name, Danny goes white.

                    ANCHOR'S VOICE
          Ilio Manzetti was one of the most respected
          and influential men in New York. As an
          investment banker, diplomat, adviser to presi-
          dents and mayors, he helped shape public
          policy and private finance for more than three
          decades. He'll be missed, Phil. This is Michael
          Port with New York 1.

Danny's knees are weak, his hands cold, his stomach rises....He
becomes aware of the others, staring at him in amazement.

                    DANNY
                    (stunned)
          Do you think I...

                    MRS. MOEBIUS
          Danny, please, we don't want to know.

She and Curtis walk out of the room. Stunned, shaken, Danny
leaves in a different direction. The TV plays to an empty room...

                    ANCHOR'S VOICE
          The assailant is described as a white male in
          his late 20s....

EXT. MOEBIUS BUILDING/STREET — DAY

Danny wanders out the door in a daze. His cell phone

RINGING. He has to search his pockets, then fumbles to turn it on....

> KYLE'S VOICE PHONE
> You finally killed a Jew, man. How's it feel?

> DANNY
> Kyle...I can't talk right now....

He hears a CAMERA SHUTTER and MOTOR DRIVE. He turns....

EXT. ACROSS THE STREET — DAY

GUY DANIELSEN & A PHOTOGRAPHER.

They're coming toward him.

> GUY
> Did you kill Ilio Manzetti?

> DANNY
> No.

Suddenly Danny runs after the photographer, they struggle.....

> PHOTOGRAPHER
> Not the camera, don't hurt the camera...

Danny opens the camera, rips out the film, exposing it.

> GUY
> Did you kill him?

Danny glares at him without answering, walks away. Guy hurries after him....

GUY

Two days ago you addressed a Nazi rally. Last week you went to a Torah study group.

DANNY

What were you, following me?

GUY

How do you reconcile the two?

DANNY

I don't. Look, stay out of what you don't understand.

GUY

Explain it so I can.

DANNY

You work for the *New York Times*. Your whole job in life is not to understand things like me.

GUY

I don't think you know what you are.

DANNY
(walking on, fast)
Yeah, and what are you? A *Times* man? A Presbyterian? Impotent? A prick?

GUY

Who killed Manzetti?

DANNY

If I tell you, will you pull the story? Not write about me?

                              GUY
              It's too late....If I didn't, somebody else would.
                         (as Danny just snorts)
              Yom Kippur starts at sundown. Will you go to
              synagogue?

                             DANNY
                      (turns on him, threatening)
              Get the fuck away from me.

Guy backs off. Danny crosses the street.

                              VOICE
              Hey, Danny, just one more!

He glances back. It's the PHOTOGRAPHER who has reloaded
and now SNAPS a shot AS DANNY TURNS AWAY and keeps
going....

EXT. LOWER MANHATTAN—DAY

Danny and Miriam walking together among the trees.

                            MIRIAM
              You're telling me you killed him? You? Killed
              him? Bullshit. What kind of gun did you use?

                            DANNY
                          (guessing)
              A forty-five.

                            MIRIAM
              It was a nine millimeter.

                            DANNY
              You're lying.

                    MIRIAM
So are you... But they'll believe you....
                    (as they walk)
Lina Moebius is saying the whole thing was
your idea. That you proposed it in a meeting
at her house.
                    (when he doesn't deny it)
Ah, Jesus, Danny...What were you thinking?
Are you glad Manzetti's dead? Do you really
want to kill Jews? You want to kill me?

                    DANNY
I was just talking. I—look, I can't help what I
think.

He doesn't know how to answer, walks away from her to the
railing overlooking the water. He stares into the current flowing
past. Finally Miriam joins him....

                    MIRIAM
All right, what if all along you were actually
infiltrating the Nazis—to expose them....

                    DANNY
But I wasn't.

                    MIRIAM
And only talked about killing Manzetti to
convince them you were an anti-Semite. If
you'd had any idea somebody would take it
seriously, you never would have said it.

                    DANNY
I can't say that.

MIRIAM

Think about your father. Your sister.

DANNY

The truth doesn't mean anything to you, does
it?

MIRIAM

Danny, I'm trying to—save you.

DANNY
(over her)

Fucking kike.

Miriam is stung. She can't believe he said that. Still, she gets a
small tape reorder out of he purse, hands it to him.

MIRIAM

Try to get Lina Moebius on tape, telling you
to do something. Something violent...That's
right, I don't care about truth. I care about
you.
(looks at her watch)
Kol Nidre's at six-thirty. I've got to meet
Stuart. We'll be at the minyan tonight and
tomorrow. If you need me, come there....

Danny watches her walk away, then turns to the railing. Ideally a
FERRY is pulling away from its slip and heading out across the
harbor. He watches it, then looks down at the current moving
past. He reaches a decision, throws the tape recorder into the
water, turns and walks away....

INT. DANNY'S APARTMENT—LATE AFTERNOON

Danny stops just inside the door. The place is spotless. The desk has been pulled out from the wall, covered with a snowy cloth and set for a Sabbath meal: brass candelabrum, challah under a satin cover...and two place settings.

Carla is pouring wine into the kiddush cup. She's wearing a modest dress, her hair is pinned up with a piece of lace.

> DANNY
> What's going on?

She turns, startled; she hadn't heard him come in.

> CARLA
> It's erev Yom Kippur....We'll have dinner, then
> go to shul. Atone for our sins.

He grabs a couple of olives off the table, eats them as he goes through his closet, stuffing a couple things in a bag....

> CARLA
> Come on, we can be like Eichmann. He
> studied Torah. He hated Jews.

> DANNY
> (in the closet, looking)
> Is it like Eichmann? Are we goofing?

> CARLA
> I don't know. I just want to try it.

> DANNY
> Shit...
> (looking in other places)
> Did you talk to your mother today?

CARLA

No. What are you looking for?

DANNY

Nothing.
          (indicates table as he keeps looking)
Why are you doing this?
                    (back to the closet)
I thought God didn't exist.

CARLA

He command its whether He exists or not...
          (off his silence; with difficulty)
Look, we can fight him and be crushed. Or we
can submit.

DANNY

          (from the closet)
And be crushed.

CARLA

Yeah, okay. But what if...what if... submitting...
being crushed, being nothing, not mattering,
what if that's the best feeling we can have?

He finds it (a kittel), stuffs it in the bag.

CARLA

Look, just light the candles with me. Then
we'll eat. You have to eat.

DANNY

You eat first, then you light.
          (exasperated, he has to explain)
Once you light, it's Yom Kippur, which means
you're fasting, so you can't...eat.

He trails off, looks at her. She's everything he ever wanted, and he's already lost her.

> DANNY
> A woman of valor, who can find her? Her
> price is above rubies....

He walks out, leaving the door open. Carla starts to call after him, but then doesn't. She turns back, lights the candles and awkwardly reads the prayers....

EXT. STREET/PAY PHONE— SUNDOWN APPROACHING

Danny on the phone. Behind him, Jews hurry home for the holiday. He hears a BEEP...

> DANNY
> Miriam, it's me, Danny....Come on, the hol-
> iday hasn't started, pick up the—
> > (as someone does)
> ...Is Stuart davening Ne'ilah tomorrow at the
> minyan...'Cause he always does...Tell him I'm
> doing it instead....

She argues (we hear her VOICE not her words)...Danny cuts her off.

> DANNY
> Miriam, I'm davening....He gives me any
> trouble, I'll beat the shit out of him right
> there in the room. I'm serious....

She's still talking when he hangs up and walks away.

INT. MOEBIUS APARTMENT—NIGHT

Lina and Curtis with Billings and Drake, who looks bad...

> LINA
> Why didn't you tell us?

> DRAKE
> (never considered it)
> I was hurt. I just...

> BILLINGS
> He went to his friends' place and I laid up
> there 'till he was better. Then he called me.

> CURTIS
> You should've gone to the police.

> LINA
> I don't think Drake wants to talk to the
> police. Do you?

> DRAKE
> I'll take care of him myself.

The phone RINGS. Curtis answers, listens, covers the mouth-
piece.

> CURTIS
> Daniel Balint.

She takes it with a dramatic gesture.

> LINA
> (takes the phone)
> Hello...?

INTERCUT WITH:

EXT. PAY PHONE, 65TH STREET—NIGHT

> DANNY
> Lina...It's happening. Tonight.

> LINA
> What is happening?

> DANNY
> Beth Shalom. Like you wanted.

> LINA
> Beth Shalom? What are you talking about?
> Who is this...?

> DANNY
> Lina, you said if I was going to plant a bomb,
> I should—

A CLICK as she hangs up. He's pleased. He steps away from the phone. He's carrying a grease-stained bag and is across from...

TEMPLE EMANU-EL...KOL NIDRE being sung by a soprano within; and ORGAN accompanying her.

EXT. 5TH AVENUE AND 65TH STREET —NIGHT

In the synagogue across the street we hear KOL NIDRE being sung by a soprano; an ORGAN accompanying her. Danny looks up at the temple.

FLASHCUT: EXT FOREST ROAD—DAY, 1943

Looking up as the Nazi sergeant holds the boy on the bayonet over the father's head. But now Danny is the father, and the father is the sergeant.

He lunges at the Nazi, knocking him down, tearing at his throat. The sergeant screams....

NAZI SOLDIER
(in German, to his fellows)

Kill him!

Danny bites through the Nazi's jugular as bullets rip into him.

INT. FIFTH AVENUE AT 65TH/INT. KYLE'S CAR—NIGHT

Kyle's car is parked on the Central Park side of Fifth....Danny gets in the passenger side. Kyle is behind the wheel, wiring an explosive device. Danny hands him the grease-stained bag.

DANNY

How're we doing?

Kyle holds up a solitary pipe bomb.

KYLE

That's all we've got left.

DANNY

It'll be enough if we use it right.
(checks his watch)
Okay, the service'll go about another hour. Say an hour for the janitors, then one more just to be safe...We'll go in at midnight.

Kyle has extracted a cheeseburger and shake from the bag. As he starts in on them, he realizes Danny isn't eating.

KYLE

Didn't you get anything?

> DANNY
> I'm not hungry....Come on, let's drive
> around....We don't want to be spotted here.

Eating, Kyle starts the car, pulls away....

INT. MOEBIUS APARTMENT — SAME TIME

> LINA
> (white with fury)
> He is trying to set us up.

Curtis picks up a cell phone and dials.

> LINA
> (to Drake and Billings)
> I want him dead by tomorrow night. That lies
> within your capacities, correct?

Billings nods. Drake unconsciously licks the center of his lower lip. As they leave, we see that he limps horribly. When they're gone...

> CURTIS
> (into phone)
> Yes, I believe that a bomb is going to be
> planted tonight at Temple Emanu-el on 65th
> Street....By the same man who killed Ilio
> Manzetti... His name is Daniel Balint....

EXT. FIFTH AVENUE/INT. KYLE'S CAR—DRIVING— NIGHT

POV inside van. Fifth is quiet. Temple Emanu-el again, straight ahead. But now we see SECURITY GUARDS near the door.

                    KYLE (V.O.)
Oh, what is this shit?

                    DANNY (V.O.)
Keep driving. Don't slow down.

                    KYLE (V.O.)
Christ...

POV speeds up, whips past the synagogue.

                    DANNY (V.O.)
Not too fast.

                    KYLE (V.O.)
You said they didn't have night guards.

                    DANNY (V.O.)
They don't. I checked twenty times.... Somebody must have talked.

                    KYLE (V.O.)
Who even knew?

                    DANNY (V.O.)
Mrs. Moebius.

                    KYLE (V.O.)
Why? Why would she?

                    DANNY (V.O.)
The Manzetti thing must have scared her. She
thinks she'll get implicated.

                    KYLE (V.O.)
So what do we with the device?

The Plaza straight ahead...

>   DANNY (V.O.)
>   Take a right on 59th...
>   (as the car turns)
>   We'll put it someplace else.

>   KYLE (V.O.)
>   Where?

ON DANNY'S FACE

>   DANNY
>   I have an idea....

INT. A DARKENED BLDG (JEWISH COMMUNITY CENTER)—NIGHT

A pencil-beam flashlight moves through the darkness. We follow it. The light enters a space where SOUND ECHOES....

>   DANNY (V.O.)
>   Over here.

INT. JEWISH COMMUNITY CENTER ROOM—NIGHT

A PENCIL BEAM shows Kyle on his back attaching the bomb to some kind of wooden floor cupboard. He's worried about the paltry amount of explosives.

>   KYLE
>   It's all reinforced in here. It's not going to
>   blow out the way we want it....

Danny is too preoccupied flipping through a machzor to answer.

                    KYLE
If I went back to that lumberyard, the guy'd
give me all the dynamite I wanted. Untrace-
able, you wouldn't—need to...

                    DANNY
No, it has to be tomorrow. You won't get this
many of them in here for another year. It'll
be fine.

                    KYLE
It's not going to be fine. It's—

                    DANNY
       Just do it.

Kyle sighs, goes about doing it, he HEARS SOMETHING and
freezes.

                    KYLE
       What's that?

Danny clicks off the light. A SILHOUETTE on the windows...

                    DANNY
       It's just somebody on the street.

Light on. Relieved, Kyle turns his attention back to the bomb.

                    KYLE
       When do you want it to go off?

                    DANNY
       Seven-thirty tomorrow evening.

KYLE

So that's what? Nineteen thirty minutes...what time is it now...

Kyle checks his wristwatch, sets the timer to eighteen hours eighteen minutes. It begins counting down.

EXT. SYNAGOGUE—NIGHT

Kyle and Danny come around the corner, get in Kyle's car parked near the side door.

EXT. EIGHTH AVENUE NEWSSTAND—NIGHT

A stack of papers, the early edition of the *Times*. As Danny grabs one, he notices a stack of tabloids....

FRONT PAGE: The Manzetti crime scene with screaming head-line: "MANZETTI SLAYER JEWISH NAZI." Next to this another tab: "JEW KILLS JEW?"

Danny grabs a *Times*, flips it over...We see only his face: registering this, unsurprised. He opens the paper....

INSERT: TWO PHOTOGRAPHS

The sweet-faced bar mitzvah boy we saw at his father's house...And a BLURRY PHOTO of Danny walking away from Guy Danielsen and the photographer outside Mrs. Moebius's house. Danny's face is not clearly seen.

TILT UP TO DANNY

Calm. He tucks the paper under his arm beside the machzor and crosses Eighth Avenue toward a cheap hotel....

CHEAP HOTEL—NIGHT
Carrying the papers, Danny goes through the door.

INT. HOTEL ROOM—EARLY MORNING

Danny at the window, staring out. The TV plays behind him.

On TV—A REPORTER INTERVIEWING MRS. MOEBIUS

> REPORTER
> ...You're saying that when he first appeared at
> your house, you had no idea he was Jewish....

> MRS. MOEBIUS
> None whatsoever. But I have to admit, I'm
> not terribly surprised.

> REPORTER
> What do you mean?

> MRS. MOEBIUS
> I think anti-semitism today is largely a Jewish
> phenomenon. Wouldn't you agree?

Danny can't help smiling at her audacity.

> REPORTER
> In the Third Reich, weren't a number of high-
> ranking Nazis of Jewish origin?

> MRS. MOEBIUS
> Yes, and they were said to be the most viru-
> lent proponents of the Final Solution. Really,
> who but a Jew would want to kill Ilio
> Manzetti simply because he was Jewish? Who
> thinks about such things?

> REPORTER
>
> The papers are going to report tomorrow that your colleague, Curtis Zampf, has been a federal informant for the past two years. Do you believe that?

> MRS. MOEBIUS
> (enigmatic smile)
>
> Curtis is always more complicated than he seems. Even now.

> REPORTER
> (to the camera)
>
> And so, on this, the most solemn day of the Jewish year, a former yeshiva student is being sought in connection with a monstrous hate crime that—

The set is CLICKED OFF with the remote. In the darkened screen, we see Danny take his bag off the bed and go out the door.

EXT. JEWISH COMMUNITY CENTER—LATE AFTERNOON

As Danny approaches, a STOCKY YOUNG MAN on a folding chair outside the front door checks him out.

> DANNY
>
> Gamar tov.

The Stocky Young Man beckons him on. As he passes, Danny spots a gun and shoulder holster inside the man's zippered jacket.

INT. JEWISH COMMUNITY CENTER—DAY

Several Yom Kippur services are going on in different rooms. And we hear different groups of VOICES. And one reading...

> VOICE
> ...They cast lots, and the lot fell on Jonah...

Danny puts on his kittel—a white prayer coat.

INT. JEWISH COMMUNITY CENTER, 2ND FLOOR/ INT. SMALL AUDITORIUM—DAY

About forty WORSHIPPERS, most in their 20s and 30s. Danny slips into the back, spots Carla up front with Miriam and Stuart. He's shocked, appalled....

CARLA—trying to follow along the prayer book, suddenly Danny is leaning over her shoulder from the row behind.

> DANNY
> (desperate whisper)
> What are you doing here?

People sitting nearby HUSH him; he ignores them.

> CARLA
> Miriam called, looking for you. She said you might come, so I...

> DANNY
> You gotta get out of here.

> CARLA
> You don't own this place.

> STUART
> Listen, Danny, you can't just barge in and—

                           DANNY

Shut up...

                          MIRIAM

You shut up. Who do you think you are?

                           DANNY
                    (to Carla, low, urgent)
There's a bomb here. It's going to go off at
seven-thirty.

                           CARLA

Oh, please...

The SHUSHING becomes louder....She turns away.

                          VOICES
        It's Yom Kippur....People are davening....Can
        you take it outside....You have some nerve....

Danny looks around at the scolding, angry, pious faces.... He hates
them. He sits back and closes his eyes.

EXT. FOREST ROAD—DAY, 1943

The Jewish father (played by Danny's father) is ripping open the
sergeant's jugular as the soldiers shoot him. One of the soldiers
(who is now Danny) says:

                    DANNY/NAZI SOLDIER
        Kill them. Kill them all.

The soldiers begin firing....But now, three Israelis commandos
appear, Danny, Avi and the security guard we saw outside. They
fire Uzis at the Nazis, who fire back.

Danny the Nazi soldier and Danny the Israeli commando fire at each other at point-blank range. The SOUND fades and we hear SCRAPING CHAIRS, MURMURS, VOICES....

INT. SMALL AUDITORIUM—SUNDOWN

Danny wakes with a start. People are about to resume after a break, but there's some confusion. People are talking to Stuart, who keeps glancing toward Danny....Danny finds his machzor and gets up...as he approaches the bema, Stuart comes to meet him.

> STUART
> Danny, listen, people expect me to daven; they
> don't want someone they don't know—leading
> the prayers.

> DANNY
> Get out of my way.

Stuart backs down. Danny steps onto the bema, opens the machzor.

> MURMURING VOICES
> What's going on?... Who is this?...I thought
> Stuart was davening....

> DANNY
> (to the room)
> Page 766

He glances at a clock at the back of the room: 6:14.

> DANNY
> Yis-gadal, v'yis-kadash sh'mey raba...

People join in, but one man, in back, is outraged.

ENRAGED MAN

Jesus Christ, you know who that is?... You see
the paper?

MALE VOICE (O.S.)
(gently teasing)
You're reading the paper on Yom Kippur, Barry?

Chuckles

ENRAGED WIFE

I saw the paper. That's not him, that guy was
darker....This is somebody else.

VOICE (O.S.)
That guy wouldn't go to shul, Barry....

ENRAGED MAN

You want to bet? I'll bet you anything...
(he's SHUSHED, "Could you, please...")
Let's go, we're leaving....

ENRAGED WIFE

Oh, for God's sake, you leave.

ENRAGED MAN

I'm going to get a cop.

He stalks to the door but doesn't leave, turns back as if compelled
to watch this outrage...as....

DANNY

Da-amiran b'alma, v'imru amen...

He begins the silent amidah, taking three steps backward, then three forward, bowing as he prays so that he sees the watch on the lectern....It says: 6:16....

DISSOLVE TO:

INT. A ROOM—SUNDOWN

Kyle on hands and knees, gasping for breath, his face bloody. DRAKE sits in a chair, injecting methamphetamine into the vein of his forearm. Billings comes through the door with a newspaper.

> BILLINGS
> I got one....

He squats beside Kyle, shows him the *Time*s story about Danny.

> KYLE
> Are you kidding me??

> BILLINGS
> Now do you know where he is?

Kyle thinks, glances at a watch: 6:47.

> KYLE
> Yeah, I bet I do.

INT. SMALL AUDITORIUM—TWILIGHT

The windoes have darkened. The congregation is on its feet chanting the AVINU MALKENU, the climactic prayer of the day.

Danny, leading the prayers, looks up at Carla, Stuart, Miriam...near the front, chanting with him. He looks at the clock: 7:21.

Suddenly it seems impossible to go through with this. He stops praying, but no one notices....

EXT. JEWISH COMMUNITY CENTER—TWILIGHT

As Kyle, Drake and Billings approach, the place seems to glow with an inner radiance. Drake and Billings hold weapons at their sides.

The stocky security guard sees them coming and gets up, reaching for his gun. Billings and Drake stop. Kyle wishes he weren't here.

Everything suspends for a moment as, within the building, three distinct GROUPS OF VOICES can be heard, each chanting the AVINU MALKENU at a slightly different point in the prayer.

Drake raises his gun and fires.

INT. JEWISH COMMUNITY CENTER—SMALL AUDITORIUM— TWILIGHT

People are chanting AVINU MALKENU so fervently that the GUNFIRE outside seems only a faint POPPING. No one particularly notices. Danny, freaking, doesn't hear the gunshots. He tries to address the people in the front rows....

> DANNY
> Wait a minute...

But the praying is too loud, too strong. No one stops or listens. He steps down off the bema....

> DANNY
> Stop praying. You've got to get out of
> here....All of you...

A few people in front are puzzled by his strange behavior, but the rest keep chanting. Stuart comes up to Danny....

                         STUART
            You wanted to daven. Now daven....

Danny glances over people's heads at the clock: 7:25. He doesn't notice...

THE DOOR

BANGS open. DRAKE stands there, .357, bleeding profusely from the head, the swastika on his lips.
At first, only a few people notice, they stop praying.

                         PEOPLE
(Panic, confusion)

            Who's that?... What is he... oh, my God...

Avi is the first one out of his chair, walks right at Drake.

                          AVI
                    (calm, forceful)
            Put down the weapon. Put it down....

Drake shoots him. Avi goes down, writhing in pain. Screams, panic. People come at Drake, but he grabs an 11-year-old girl, puts the gun to her head.

                         DANNY
            Drake! Up here...

Everyone turns, including Drake—who's blinded by the blood in his eyes, but recognizes the voice.

ENRAGED MAN
See, he knows him. The Nazi bastard...

Drake moves unsteadily toward the front, pulling the girl with him. A WOMAN (a doctor) goes to tend Avi, who is still conscious. People begin to slip out the back, taking children. Others stay, looking to jump Drake, but he keeps the .357 on the little girl.

DANNY
(to Carla, Miriam, Stuart)
Get everybody out of here. Fast.

He steps back onto the bema, separating himself from the others and drawing Drake's attention. The clock reads 7:28. Outside we begin to hear SIRENS....

DANNY
Drake...

Drake refocuses, pulls the girl on....From the hall, we hear OTHER GROUPS in the building, chanting....

VOICES
Avinu malkenu, choney-nu v'aneyenu...
Avinu malkenu, choney-nu v'aneyenu, ki eyn
banu ma-asim...
(Our father, our king, graciously answer us
though we are undeserving...)
—nu va-aneynu...

At the front, Drake wobbles. People start forward. He cocks the gun against the little girl's head. She's weeping silently.

DANNY
Drake, I'm right here....

Drake looks. Danny reaches out a hand. Drake points the .357 at him and FIRES, missing. A HAND grabs the little girl, pulls her to safety.

The room is nearly empty now, save Miriam, Carla, Stuart, a few others. The AVINU MALKENU can still be heard from the hall....

> ENRAGED MAN
> (from the door)
> Let them kill each other. They're animals.

> ENRAGED WIFE
> Barry, for God's sake...

Drake wobbles from loss of blood. Nearly drops the .357.

Danny glances at the clock: 7:30. What is it, another dud??

Drake FIRES again, hits Danny in the shoulder....

> CARLA
> Danny!

She runs forward. The shoulder hurts; he calls to the others....

> DANNY
> GET HER OUT OF HERE!

Miriam, others, grab Carla, pull Carla toward the door.

Drake comes toward Danny, trying to lift the .357 for the kill.

> VOICES
> Cha'nainu v'anainu, ki ain baw-nu ma'ah-
> seem...

Danny grabs Drake's gun hand, forces it up in the air. The gun goes off. Plaster rains down on them.

Drake dies. Danny catches him under the arms.

He looks at the watch: 7:32. He relaxes.

> VOICES
> (fervent)
> ...Asey imanu tz'dakah va'chesed...Asey imanu tz'dakah va'chesd, v'ho-shi—

The instant before the prayer ends...it's cut off by a sudden silence. Then a FLASH of light...

The SCREEN GOES WHITE...

> CARLA'S VOICE
> Danny, no...

INT. STAIRCASE, YESHIVA—DAY

Where we saw Danny leave the school as a 12-year-old. Now LOOKING DOWN, we see Danny as an adult, coming up them two at a time.

FOLLOWING DANNY as he races up. His old teacher, RAV ZINGESSER, appears on a landing above....

> RAV ZINGESSER
> Danny, good to see you...I wanted to take up
> that discussion we were having...
> (as Danny hurries past)
> ...about Abraham and Isaac

> DANNY
> I can't right now....

But as he nears the NEXT LANDING, there is Zingesser waiting for him again...

> ZINGESSER
>
> You remember what you said, that Isaac actually died on Mt. Moriah? I've been thinking maybe you were right...Died yet was reborn in olam ha-bah....

Danny goes past once more....

But now, LOOKING DOWN at Zingesser as he appears above Danny yet again. As Danny nears the landing...

> ZINGESSER
>
> Danny, stop...
>   (as Danny goes by, calling after him)
> ...Where are you going?... Don't you know, there's nobody up there?

As Danny passes the camera we PAN to watch him still racing upward, beyond us into the darkness....

THE END

Screenplay Notes

Henry Bean

pp 25-29 **Yeshiva scene.**
This longish scene, which opens the screenplay but not the film, was a late addition. [I had intended to begin on the subway, shocking the audience with Danny's attack (physical and verbal) on the yeshiva student. I wanted to start with an unforgivable act, then seduce the audience, against its will, into sympathizing with someone it hated.]

However, many early readers of the screenplay complained that they could not understand how and why Danny had become a Nazi. This material did not really interest me, in fact, seemed irrelevant. I thought of his Nazism as a mystery too deep for explanation, on the one hand, and, on the other, as so obvious it didn't need one. As Paul Hond would later say, this was not so much a movie about a Jewish Nazi as simply about being Jewish. Indeed, the young Orthodox males to whom I showed early drafts of Danny's anti-Semitic diatribes were stunningly blasé about them: "Yeah, yeah,"they shrugged, "I used to think that stuff."

But out of Hollywood habit and the fact that one of the complainers was a potential investor, I wrote the yeshiva scene. I liked its old-fashioned clunkiness and was satisfied that it helped understand Danny without explaining him. I liked especially that when we jumped ten years to the subway, the audience wouldn't be sure which boy was Danny—the yeshiva student or the neo-Nazi beating him up —since that was the point: in a way, he was both.

But when we began to edit the film, the yeshiva didn't work as an opening. It was too long, too low-key, too talky. Worst of all, it domesticated Danny and made it too easy to like him. Now one knew from the start that he was a Jew and all his problems with religion became simply arguments with the rabbis.

So I went back to the original idea; open on the train. And when the yeshiva was broken into bits and scattered them like memories through the film, it played better than it had in one big chunk.

p. 26 **"HaShem."** Literally "the name,"a less sacred name of G-d, usable in everyday discourse in a way that the holier ones are not.

p. 27 **Shalom Spiegel.** *The Last Trial: The Akedah,* Woodstock,VT.: Jewish Lights Publishing, 1993.

p. 32 **Danny gets call from a woman. Danny orders vegetarian takeout.**

I imagined that prior to Carla, Danny had exclusively one-night stands; sex was necessary, relationships were impossible.

The vegertarianism is, of course, a reference to Hitler, but also to Jews who keep kosher. The question about soup stocks is typical of observant Jews ordering in restaurants. In fact, Danny goes beyond either Hitler or the Orthodox; he's a vegan. Both of these conversations were cut from the finished film.

pp 33-34 **Vompadink**. This scene and the following two were shot and then cut. In the finished film, Danny, Billings, Carleton and O.L. arrive at Mrs. Moebius's house as if they were old friends. There was a real Vompadink, a bar in Yorktown (east 80s) reputed to be owned by a former U-boat captain, and, thus, a hangout for old Nazis. We rented another bar in Williamsburg for the location and we hadn't the time or the money to make a new sign.

pp 41-42 **The litany of famous Jews** ("...Leona Helmsley, Michael Eisner...") was meant as an homage to Alan Sherman's comedy routine in "My Son, the Folksinger."But the list of names grew shorter (and less funny) with each draft and was edited out of the final film, along with other bits and pieces of dialogue.

pp 43-44 The pieces of this scene were rearranged not in the editing, but on the set. The location had no place in which to plausibly stage Lina and Curtis's conversation about Danny while he was still present, so we redid the blocking and had that occur at the top of the stairs just after he's left. This constitutes a small violation of point of view, one of the only times in the film in which there is dialogue to which Danny is not privy.

pp 49-50 **EXT. STREET CORNER** This scene was never shot. The schedule was so tight that we cut any scene that wasn't absolutely necessary to the story. Losing it cost us some complexity in Danny's relations with the other skinheads.

p. 50 **The quotation from Hoffmansthal** (a German Jew) was suggested by Silke Weinick, a friend who teaches German literature at the University of Michigan.

p. 51 **The reference to Carla's father coming from Argentina**

was an attempt to explain Summer Phoenix's olive complexion. Her mother is Jewish.

pp 52-53 Carla sobbing, then turns to Danny for more sex.
We shot this scene on the first day, and on the morning of the second day I woke up thinking that I'd put the camera in the wrong place. I'd had it by the window, looking across the bed at Danny and Carla. Now, it seemed, it should have been down low, looking up at Carla's bruised and sobbing face (a semiprivate moment), which would have then allowed her to turn away from the camera and play the subsequent "let's have sex again"moment offscreen. When I got to the set the second day and explained the new idea, we all agreed we'd redo it, if not at this location, then at another. We never did, and the entire piece got cut. And every subsequent day, I woke up to another similar thought of what I'd done wrong and would never get a chance to do right.

p. 55 Danny in the basement, looks through a box of his old stuff. The yeshiva memory that occurs here in the film was not planned, but invented during the editing.

p. 59 Not like Mr. Dorfmann."Mr. Dorfmann was imagined to be a neighbor of the family, but early audiences were confused—had there once been a comedian named Mr. Dorfmann? So I went back to an earlier version of the line, "Not like your Uncle Mitch,"and we laid this in during ADR.

"**After your mother died,**"etc. This piece of dialogue is the only thing that I actively regret cutting from the film. It is a bit expositional, but I like acknowledging the mother's death, and I love Danny's switch from the personal to baseball, and that the father follows without missing a beat. It says a lot about their relationship. Another mistake.

pp 61-71 **The coffee shop.** This was the first scene I wrote, and is the one scene in the film that actually comes from the historical incident of Daniel Burros, though the actual content of the scene is original to the film.

p. 71 **As Danny walks out of the coffee shop,** the film cuts to a memory: Danny, at 12, going down the yeshiva stairs after he's been thrown out of class. This, too, was "written"during the editing.

pp 78-79 **Danny on the phone with Carla.** The technical difficulties involved in photographing Danny on the phone while recording both sides of the conversation were too much for us. (Especially with the actress out of town because she didn't work that week.) We ended up recording them separately, which never really worked, so the scene was cut. Too bad, I thought this could have been funny.

p. 80 **The American Nazis that Danny Burros belonged to actually had a dog named Gas Chamber.** I desperately wanted him in the film, but of the two dogs we lined up, one turned out to be a biter, and the other bailed on us after we'd changed its shoot day too many times. Alas, poor Gas Chamber...

p. 86 **Flashback to the Nazi era.** Originally, this scene was to be set at the entrance to a concentration camp. I was nervous about depicting the camps at all, but was spared that problem by the fact that we didn't have enough money to create them. We considered using a railroad yard and dressing a couple of boxcars to look like 1942 Poland, but even that proved impossible. Finally someone suggested a horsedrawn cart in the same woods where we were already shooting the skinheads' country "retreat." The horse was what sold me. I thought of Auden's "Musée des Beaux Arts"and "the executioner's horse" who flicks flies with its tail, oblivious to the slaughter of humans going on all around him.

pp 86-88 **The ending to this scene** was written just before shooting at the insistence and inspiration of Susan Hoffman. Susan (who produced the film with Chris Roberts) rarely insists, but she felt that, in acting terminology, Danny had to "lose"the scene, and the Rumanian woman had to win it. She was certainly right, and not just for this scene, but for the way in which that loss helped to set up the beginnings of Danny's conversion in the desecration scene that will follow.

pp 91-96 and pp 100-101. **All of this material** was severely trimmed and moved up earlier during the editing. The construction of this "country"portion of the film was one of the most difficult parts of the editing.

pp 96-100 **These scenes of Danny going to say kaddish for his mother**, but refusing or unable to enter the temple, were cut. We first considered to save time and money, but once I thought about it, I became convinced that they undercut the more important "desecration scene"to come. If Danny could already go to a synagogue and say kaddish, how surprised would we be when he found himself "unexpectedly"moved by the santury, the ark and the Torahs. I liked this scene, but it stepped on the more important one. It had to go.

p. 100 **Danny watches Carla making love to Curtis.** It is much easier to write this stuff than to direct it. The people who do these things on the page are entirely imaginary; the actors who have to take off their clothes and pretend to do them in front of camera are human beings. Everyone's collective embarrassment makes it hard to focus on the objective details of getting the scene right.

pp 100-101 **This scene of Curtis talking to Danny** was moved from the "defunct motel" to Mrs. Moebius's house because of actor's scheduling issues.

pp 111 **Ein sof** means, literally, "without end." I had the rabbi deliberately add the mistranslation "nothingness without end" to pick up the phrase Danny had used in the interview with Guy Daniels (scene 27). There Danny is using it to denigrate "the Jews," and here he finds that it is the name of God in His most ineffable incarnation. Piety continually pursues and overtakes his apostasy.

p. 112 Here, in the script, **Danny wraps himself in the tallis** and says the Alenu. In the film he says, *"V'zot ha-torah..."* the beginning of the phrase sung in shul when the Torah is lifted up after it has been read from. Some Jews will point a pinkie finger at the uplifted scroll, and we combined that with a Nazi salute.

pp 116-117 **Dumping the van.** Day after day we put this scene on the shooting schedule, and day after day we didn't get to it. Finally we repeated the scene on the yeshiva stairs, then cut to a second unit shot of the East River for the transition back to New York.

p. 120 **In the script the scene ends with a joke** that was shot but cut out of the film. We thought Lina Moebius would be too touchy about violence even to joke about it. And, as the reader will see, an entire subplot involving Drake coming to take revenge was taken out of the movie.

p. 121 One of my favorite moments: **Carla kissing the vomit off Danny's face.** The reference was to St. Francis kissing the leper.

pp 127-128 **The recurring "flashbacks" to the "real Nazis"** and Danny's imagined elaborations of the Polish man's story, read all right in the script, but seemed laboriously obvious in the film. Still, the jumps to and back from that reality gave the film a boost. So Lee Percy, our second editor, abstracted these moments, taking out most of the narrative content. Jim Denault had wanted to shoot these scenes in black and white; I finally opted for color, then went back to black and white in the editing. It would have been better to do it Jim's way in the first place.

pp 136-139 **My favorite scene,** largely because I finally overcame the sound department's insistence that I not let the actors step on each other's lines, which meant no natural interruptions. Here I shot the scene in a master that included everyone and rehearsed them to deliver the lines as quickly as possible. The result is the closest the film comes in dialogue to the comic timing I wanted, and I especially like the way that pace makes the relative complexity of what's being said almost, but not quite, impossible to follow.

pp 160-161 This scene begins a complex subplot that was shot, but has been entirely cut out of the finished film. The wounded Drake returns, accompanied by Billings and seeking vengeance; it is he, of course, who has killed Ilio Manzetti. Mrs. Moebius sees how she might use this to distance the group from Danny (recently revealed as unstable, possibly Jewish). Meanwhile...

pp 161-162 **...Danny pretends that Mrs. Moebius has told him to blow up Temple Emanu-el** (the big synagogue on 5th Avenue). The thinking here is so overly intricate I'm surprised we ever thought it would work. The idea is that by seeming to frame Lina for the anticipated bombing, she will call the police to warn them (protecting herself) and, thus, when he and Kyle drive by Temple Emanu-el, where they'd intended to plant the bomb, there will now be cops and security, so they'll have to deviate to plan B, the little shul where Danny has already arranged that he'll be leading the Ne'ilah service, which concludes Yom Kippur.

pp 177-178 **More of the Drake plot;** he and Billings find Kyle who, beaten and shown the day's *Times*, finally believes that Danny is a Jew and then realizes where he must be.

p. 179 In the film, Danny's conscience gets all the congregants out of the shul to save them. In the script, he has the same moral impulse, begins to do the same thing, but is interrupted by Drake, who, wounded in his gun battle outside with the security guard, bursts in here mortally wounded, shoots Avi and grabs the little girl for protection. But what he really wants is Danny, and the rest of the scene orchestrates everyone else leaving the room, then Danny and Drake battling, Drake's death, then, just when we think that this bomb, too, might not go off, it does.

Despite Glenn Fitzgerald's brilliance as Drake, I did not stage this action very well; more important, for much of the audience Drake was a confusing element. The "thriller ending"clashed with the rest of the film, particularly with what seemed strongest in it. I had rather liked the confusion, the seeming contradiction, but as soon as Lee Percy edited Drake out of this scene, people understood the film better and were more moved by the ending. The argument was irresistible.

pp 180-181 This wonderful scene was conceived by Leora Barish, radically simplifying the overly long and complex epilogue that I had written.

The Believer in
the Cultural
Marketplace

Adapted from *The Independent*

Beth Pinsker

H enry Bean welcomes controversy, but the way his film has been received is something different. *The Believer* won the grand jury prize at Sundance and then catapulted the director into a Hollywood maelstrom that has left Bean without a major theatrical distributor.

The process started normally enough. After Sundance, Bean went to Los Angeles to sell the film and he showed it to staff at the Simon Wiesenthal Center, curators of Los Angeles's Museum of Tolerance. This kind of screening has become more than a courtesy in the entertainment world. Filmmakers with work about gays show it to GLAAD, those with work about blacks run it past the NAACP, and those with work about Jews show it to the Wiesenthal Center or the Anti-Defamation League.

There are no guarantees that the result will always be positive, though. Rabbi Abraham Cooper, the assistant dean of the Wiesenthal Center, didn't like *The Believer*. "This film did not work," he told the *Los Angeles Times* after the issue became public. Potential distributors fled, for unstated reasons. Bean was flabbergasted. "I blithely went over there to show this film, thinking they would see it for what it was, an obvious paean to Judaism," he says. But like a film that can't ever get its legs because its first weekend is slow, Bean says, "It was too late. It was like the first weekend was bad in the Jewish world."

Bean did slightly better with the Anti-Defamation League, but still the tone was muted. "While many may find it objectionable," the ADL said in an official statement on the film, "the filmmaker succeeds in his portrayal of this disturbing subject without legitimizing or glamorizing the hate-filled protagonist, anti-Semitism, or the lifestyle of skinheads."

Critics tried to plead the filmmaker's cause. In *Entertainment Weekly*, Lisa Schwartzbaum took the space she would have used to review *Town and Country* (which didn't end up having a press screening) to trumpet the film as a "unique feature film aflame with vivid depictions of the wages of brutish hate."

"Far worse films have been backed. Why make such a big deal about this?" she asks.

The film hasn't exactly died on the festival circuit, like so many other films labeled "difficult" or "not commercial," but it won't go as far as most celebrated Sundance films either. Bean sold his film to Showtime, where it was set to premiere in September as part of the pay cable network's "No Limits" campaign. A few months later, IDP, the distribution arm associated with the film's production company, Fireworks Pictures, was going to stage a theatrical release. But *The Believer*'s route to the screen—both small and large—got even more circuitous after the events of September 11, 2001. The film was part of the Contemporary World Cinema selection at the Toronto International Film Festival, which was just half over when the terrorist attacks occurred. *The Believer* was to have its first public screening that night. It was cancelled, and Showtime subsequently pushed back the film's air date from September 30 until March, delaying the theatrical release until the late spring or early summer. While many films and television shows delayed their premieres at the same time, Showtime was particularly concerned about the content in *The Believer* and how it would be received in a post-attack world. "In order to be sensitive to the current mood of our country, we feel that it would be appropriate to delay the broadcast to a time when our audience might be more receptive to this kind of strong drama," a Showtime spokesperson said at the time. Whenever *The Believer* ends up making it's debut, this Sundance winner will only be eligible for the Emmys, not the Oscars, Independent Spirits, or other film awards.

"Even though the picture is one of highest profile available as an acquisition, a lot of people found it easier to say no," says Bob Aaronson, vice president of acquisitions at Fireworks. "With the

USAs and Searchlights today, they don't have the appetite for anything challenging. But they're all difficult."

What exactly is it about this film that it was too much for a company like Miramax, which released Antonia Bird's *Priest on Easter,* or Sony Pictures Classics, which released the similarly controversial *In the Company of Men*?

The issue is not about a Jew turning into a neo-Nazi, despite how controversial that simple description sounds. People now generally understand the psychological concept of identifying with the aggressor. And Bean's premise is based on the true story of Daniel Burros, a KKK grand dragon who committed suicide in 1965 after the *New York Times* reported that he was Jewish.

It's not about Bean himself. The first question people ask is if he's Jewish—just to make sure. (For better or worse, it would be a whole different kind of controversy if a non-Jew made a film like this.) And he is, in fact. He's a Reform Jew from Philadelphia who now lives in New York.

It isn't even about the anti-Semitism that the main character spouts, or his desecrating a Torah (no actual Torah was harmed in the filming). The Wiesenthal Center got behind *American History X*, in which Edward Norton portrayed a charismatic neo-Nazi, though it depicted similar savagery. It even showed the film at its museum to teach young kids about hate.

What Rabbi Cooper and others respond to is something intangible in the film's tone, which people read differently depending on their backgrounds. For some all it signals is that others are going to find it controversial, while they don't themselves—"all I got at first were constant predictions of controversy to come, without encountering any of the controversy," Bean says. For those others it creates an immediate visceral reaction that can often be negative.

"I think some viewers will be fearful that, in the wrong hands, *The Believer* might justify or provoke violence," says Annette Insdorf, director of undergraduate studies at Columbia University and author of *Indelible Shadows: Film and the Holocaust*. Insdorf was impressed by the acting and thought the film "compelling, thought-provoking, and tautly directed." She also found the film disturbing in that there is so much detail left out. "What happened in the intervening decade or so between the flashback in the classroom and his avowed desire to kill Jews?" she asks. "How was he affected by his (absent) mother or his all-too-briefly presented father? Because it raises more questions than it answers, there is an unsatisfying feeling at the end."

In the film world, the situation is much like what happened with *In the Company of Men* at Sundance four years prior.

"We get into cultural debates every year at Sundance," says the festival's director, Geoff Gilmore, citing Errol Morris's *Mr. Death and Sex: The Annabel Chong Story*. "What's different about *The Believer* and *In the Company of Men* is that they are literally about an exploration of the phenomenon [of racism or sexism]. With *The Believer*, it's about that crisis of cultural identity, which is a universal subject, and of this very particular self-loathing of Jews that has been a tradition of Jewish art and literature."

This self-hating or even just bare exploration of religion happens to be one of the most touchy subjects in American Judaism today. Bean's film takes it to an extreme, but if Danny Balint had merely gone from being a yeshiva student to eating bacon cheeseburgers—while expressing the same ambivalent emotions about his upbringing and God—the filmmaker might have enraged the same groups of people.

The character gets deep into this debate throughout the movie. At one point, he's arguing with an old classmate at synagogue. Avi, who doesn't know Danny really is a skinhead, calls him a Jewish Nazi because Danny thinks Jews are wimps. Danny fires back that Zionists are Nazis.

"They're racist, militaristic, and act like storm troopers in the territories," Danny says.

An older woman standing with them sizes up the situation in a snap and asks Danny pointedly, "Do you hate them because they're wimps or because they're storm troopers? Or do you just hate them?"

In just one exchange, Bean has riled up about seven different ongoing theological and moral debates within the Jewish community —self-hatred, the treatment of the Palestinians in Israel, the goals of Zionism, assimilation, ultra-Orthodoxy, Holocaust obsession and talking in synagogue.

Then, too, there's the ending to deal with, which is always crucial in a film that is supposed to make a cultural point. Jewish groups endorsed *American History X,* essentially, because by the conclusion of the film the neo-Nazi sees the error of his ways. One of Rabbi

Cooper's chief criticisms of *The Believer* is about where it leads. He doesn't see a pedagogic line that eventually dispels the character's anti-Semitic rants. Instead, it appears that the character is sanctified in spite of his beliefs; he's destroyed in the end, but it seems that it's as a martyr and not in retribution.

"The only way I can rationalize the story is to look closely at the opening and the closing, which invoke Abraham's binding of Isaac," says Insdorf. "The frame of *The Believer* is about God testing man, while Danny seems to be testing God: How far can Danny go before being stopped? A sacrifice is the answer."

"I didn't think it was finally about self-hatred," Bean argues. "The character had ambivalence, I felt. He loves Judaism just as much as he hates it." And whether or not he is destroyed in the end, has a hand in his own destruction, returns to Judaism, or defies until the end, is up in the air. Bean knows what he thinks, but realizes that people will read the film as they want.

"There is this dynamic, it's there throughout the film, and some people will get it in vast detail. Some will have a feeling that they can't articulate," he says.

All of this, however, may be too fine a Talmudic point for most viewers. In fact, much of the philosophical debate about the film may be too detailed for those who aren't schooled in the Yom Kippur prayers or the commentaries on the binding of Isaac.

Matthew Duda, Showtime's executive vice president of program acquisitions and planning, is not a Torah scholar. What he does know is dealing with controversial films. His network's responsible for the gay series *Queer as Folk* as well as the acquisition of Angelica Huston's *Bastard Out of Carolina*, which Ted Turner wouldn't let New Line release because the child abuse it depicted was too graphic, and Adrian Lyne's *Lolita*, which no American distributor would touch because of the sexual content.

"Premium cable has become the place to handle difficult material," Duda says. In fact, premium cable needs difficult material in order to separate itself from the pack and get people to pay a monthly fee for access. Duda needs not only to scoop HBO on provocative material, but also network TV, basic cable, and the weekend movies. What could be better for that than premiering a film that nobody else will touch?

The way Duda builds up a film like *The Believer* is through a steady marketing campaign, with review tapes for influential critics and on-air promotions and advisories. Duda makes use of the channel's Web site [www.sho.com] to supply additional material and chat opportunities. He also has the option of putting together a special discussion after the film, either for air or in private, so that people can discuss the issues that the film raises. If all finally goes well, the film will score decent ratings on its opening night, live on in replays and on video and help cement Showtime's reputation for daring.

"'No Limits' doesn't mean there's not programming we wouldn't put on the air," Duda says. "We want high quality entertainment that's dramatic as well as funny. There's always somebody out there saying you shouldn't do lots of things. That's what our free society gives us. Lively debate, we welcome it."

Duda also has the option of trying to get community support before a show airs by scheduling special screenings for groups like the Wiesenthal Center—except, of corse in this particular case.

This process of drumming up support from an interested community isn't exactly new, but it has never before been so entrenched and so public. Scott Seomin, entertainment media director of GLAAD, traces it back to when his group had success boycotting *Basic Instinct* in 1992, and says it has been growing ever since.

The Wiesenthal Center's Rabbi Cooper says he's been asked for years for help on various projects, but only as a way to try to avoid offensive images or historical inaccuracies and not as an effort in censorship or political correctness.

"Nobody has to come to us to pass muster," he says. "It's usually very minor input, like making sure the number of people who died in a concentration camp is correct. In 24 years, and including *The Believer*, I've never picked up a phone to say to somebody in the industry not to make a film."

Showtime might have had more luck using the director to go out there and explain his film. An articulate filmmaker can, in a sense, sooth any nerves that might get jangled market by market. This is what Neil LaBute did when some critics accused *In the Company of Men* of misogyny and tagged the director with the same motives as his characters. LaBute explained what he was trying to do in the film—talking about the psychological exploration of evil—and more and more critics started to get it and like the film as a result. The little details about LaBute being a nice guy and a practicing Mormon didn't hurt either.

Yet, although Bean doesn't stonewall either about his Jewish upbringing or his own feelings about religion, he doesn't want his background and his motives to get too confused with the meaning of the film. "Whatever I am," he says, "the film remains what it is."

He thinks that too many personal details about a director can be distracting. "It clouds your own personal reaction to it. If I'm proud of one thing in this film, it's that we threw a million things in there and didn't sort it out for you." With *In the Company of Men*, he says if people were comforted knowing that LaBute was a Mormon—in the sense that it made him seem wholesome—they would see the film through a different moral prism. And that's too easy. "The scary and exciting thing about that film is being able to read your own thing into it," he says.

For the same reasons, Bean, as well as others like Sundance's Gilmore, worries about the effect community groups will have on free speech if they scare potential distributors into thinking that films do have to pass some sort of-political correctness test—no matter if the group's true intent is just to inform. If the idea of sending studio product past community groups is relatively new, imagine their shock at having to send something like *The Believer*. Directors still getting used to the attention and freedom of the indie film boom are suddenly up against a new kind of conformity.

"Characters that come out of some of these films give a sense of something that's breaking molds and that deals with different kinds of aspects of identity. People could look at this and say, 'You can't portray this in this way,'" Gilmore says.

Bean thinks the more edgy independent films might be in danger of getting cut off under this new system of checks. Distributors, he says, "are scared of the prospect of negative publicity. At one of the places, a publicist said to me, 'I can market the hell out of this film.' The truth is, the studio decided it's nothing compared to damage they might incur if organized Jewish groups decided to take it out."

The result of this pressure, Bean says, is that "the studio movie business—even on the art-house level—is always being pushed toward lowest common denominator. We get the blandest version of everything, and that becomes more and more our culture."

Self-Criticism
in Public

David Kraemer

The *Believer* is a film with the power to evoke strong emotions. There is something in this story that touches a tender nerve, particularly if the viewer is a Jew. How else might we explain the condemnation of *The Believer* by one rabbi, who described it as "a primer for anti-Semitic actions," given that nothing it portrays is unavailable to the curious thug on a myriad of extremist Web sites. Or the reaction of a viewer in Israel who exploded in anger, criticizing various small details in the film with an emotion totally out of proportion with the nature of the criticism. The film's main character, Danny, is unavoidably provocative. But it is not immediately obvious what about him has this power. What makes him, and the film that is his vehicle, so successfully troubling?

Undoubtedly, part of the answer is Danny's hateful brutality. From the very first scene in the film, we know Danny as a violent bully. And his verbal bullying is often more brutal than his physical. For some viewers, this is disturbing enough. But movies today are filled with violence, often far more extreme than that depicted here. And the representation of bigoted thugs often makes us feel not troubled but smug and superior; "I could never be like that," we say to ourselves in a self-congratulatory tone. But Danny doesn't allow us to respond with such easy superiority, for it is not obvious—to some of us, at least—that "we could never be like that." Or, to be more accurate, even if we could never imagine *doing* what Danny does, we could imagine *feeling* as he feels. It is this, I would argue, that ultimately makes his provocation so powerful.

It would not be difficult to imagine a version of *The Believer* that failed to provoke. Had Danny been a simple self-hating Jew, extreme but unnuanced, the story might have offered mere exploitation—some violence and sex, but little of enduring interest. Had Danny acted out of a blind desire to eradicate self and people, his character would have been repugnant and the film a forgettable curiosity. What makes *The Believer* so impressively compelling as narrative and important as commentary is the Danny who both hates and loves his Jewishness, and provides equally good reasons for *both*. The underlying reasonableness of both sides of Danny's ambivalence is what allows his character to transcend the mundane. If Danny's affection for the tradition of his ancestors alone made sense, then this film would have been a grand act of pandering. It is because Danny's anger also commands consideration that the thoughtful viewer cannot repress *The Believer* from consciousness.

What is the source of Danny's venom toward Judaism and Jews? There are perhaps personal motivations, reasons in his individual history that turn him against the faith of his father(s). Surely we can feel frustrated, even infuriated, with the passive, pathetic figure who is Danny's father. But this would be a weak—because unelaborated—foundation. If there is one complaint I have heard repeatedly from others who have seen the film, it is the absence of any dynamic explorations of Danny's psychology or character. The youthful Danny we see early in the film is already a magnificent critic of the tradition, one whose criticism borders on rage. How did he get to be this way? We have little way of knowing. Certainly the declining father of later years cannot offer a sufficient explanation. So it is not a complex, richly detailed biography that explains Danny's anger. In fact, it seems to me that Danny's anger is not personal at all. The absence of the personal suggests that what he expresses is not his own. It is, as a conceptualization of both history and theology, an expression of anger on behalf of the Jewish people as a whole. What Danny gives voice to is what any Jew might say—if he could allow himself.

Consider Danny's debate with his teacher in the yeshiva classroom. The discussion focuses on the well-known story of the binding of Isaac by his father Abraham (called the "Akedah" in Jewish tradition; see Genesis, chapter 22). Danny challenges the Torah's narrative, or at least his teacher's representation of it, in virtually every detail. To the Torah's command that Abraham take his "only son," Danny responds that Abraham had another son, Ishmael. When his classmate, Avi, explains that Isaac was the only son whom Abraham loved, Danny responds sarcastically, "Oh, they only kill them when they love them...?" He then characterizes the God of the story as a bully. When his teacher rebukes him for judging God, Danny responds that God gave us free will and intelligence, and our exercise of judgment must therefore be the will of God. He then heightens his protest by declaring that Abraham actually killed Isaac. And even if he didn't, Danny observes, Isaac was so traumatized by the event that he was as good as dead for the rest of his life.

Danny, in this scene, is hardly the conventional pious "yeshiva bocher." His angry challenge will not be turned aside. But, in this respect, he surely goes no further than might any modern person who has read the biblical story. Who has not wondered about the nature of the God who stands behind the cruel command that Abraham sacrifice his son? What modern Jew has not tried to rationalize or suppress the simple meaning of the Torah's starkly troubling narrative? The moment one allows for critical questioning, as anyone participating in modern culture must, one cannot help but observe what Danny observes. If Danny is extreme in this scene, it is only for his unwillingness to avert his critical gaze.

Or consider the characterizations offered by the adult Danny to Guy, the *New York Times* reporter, in the café. Explaining the perversity—sexual and otherwise—of the Jews, Danny argues that "a people—a real people—derives its genius from the land: the sun, the sea, the soil. This is how they know themselves. But the Jew doesn't have soil." Asked about the Israelis, Danny responds that "those aren't real Jews.... They no longer need Judaism because they have soil. The real Jew is a wanderer, a nomad. He has no roots, no attachments. So he universalizes everything." In this exchange, Danny begins as a modern romantic, espousing the very ideas that would energize early Zionism in the nineteenth century. Is it not true that there is something abnormal about the condition of a people without a land? We will each have our own response to this question. But Jewish heroes of the last century certainly thought this to be so. And the flip side of Danny's argument, claiming that Israelis are not "real Jews" because "real Jews" are landless and universalist, is merely a slightly edgy articulation of Franz Rosenzweig's praise of "the people in exile." The Jewish journey across the continents has not been an entirely negative legacy. Jews and Judaism have been enriched by the need to learn to live in multiple civilizations. So, is it a good thing that Jews have once again built a particularist society on their own soil? Not a few liberal Jews have wondered about this. And is the secular "macho" Israeli really a Jew? A recent photographic exhibit at the Jewish Museum in New York, picturing a macho Israeli in military dress and tefillin (prayer straps), asks this question without offering a clear answer. Danny is, in other words, in good modern Jewish company.

In other scenes, Danny expresses what other Jews might express if only they could permit themselves. In his confrontation with the elderly survivors of the Holocaust as part of his sensitivity training, Danny's lack of sympathy (until the last moment) is appalling. But who can dismiss his question to the man who watched the murder of his son—"What did you do while the sergeant was killing your son?" Is it not true that centuries of persecution left Jews in Europe with a legacy of passivity that was self-destructive? Has Israel not learned the lesson implicit in Danny's question and refused to let itself stand by while its children are murdered? Danny is not wrong and his anger is understandable. If he is pitiless in the way he expresses his critique, he is also too candid for the contemporary Jew to hear the truth in what he speaks.

Of a similar quality is Danny's rant before the invited audience, arguing that to destroy the Jew one must love the Jew. "The Jew wants to be hated," he suggests provocatively. "He longs for our scorn. He clings to it as if it were the very core and mystery of his being. If Hitler had not existed, the Jews would have invented him. For without such hatred, the so-called Chosen People would vanish from the earth." However perverse Danny's formulation of his argument here, there is something very right in what he claims. How else might one explain the continued fund-raising success of the Anti-Defamation League when, by all objective accounts, anti-Semitism is at an all-time low in this country? Or how, in the same context, can we understand the relatively high rate of affirmative answers by Jews to survey questions asking whether "anti-Semitism is a serious/very serious problem in this country?" I have a rabbi friend who has claimed—in private conversation—that "our real problem is that they want to sleep with us, not that they want to kill us." And believe me, my friend the rabbi is no anti-Semite. Even Danny's claim that Jews would have invented Hitler, while perhaps wrong in the specifics, is not entirely off base. The Jews who answer "yes" to the "serious problem" question are inventing anti-Semites in their imaginations every day. Besides, according to universal scholarly opinion, Haman, in the biblical book of Esther, is a fictional character. So if Jews did not invent Hitler, we did invent Haman. The problem with Danny's argument, in this instance, is only in the details.

So if Danny does not always speak *the* truth, he generally speaks *a* truth, and his is almost always a truth with ample modern Jewish support. Furthermore, his argument often has a pedigree that extends well back into Jewish tradition. For example, his exchange with his teacher over God's command that Abraham sacrifice Isaac replicates, in many of its details, precisely the questions that Rashi, the paramount medieval Jewish commentator, articulates at the very same points. "Take your son," says God; "I have two sons," says Rashi, putting words in Abraham's mouth. "Your only son," says God; "each is unique to his mother," says Rashi. "The one whom you love," says God; "I love both of them," says Rashi, again for Abraham. Danny is a genuine yeshiva-bocher, one who argues often, if not always, from within the tradition. It might outrage the modern secular Jew to learn that Abraham might in fact have killed Isaac. But the educated Danny knows that one midrashic tradition represents exactly that version of the story. And, far better than his teacher, Danny knows that there is no reason not to follow that midrash. It is recorded in the canonical tradition and is therefore a legitimate view.

So what is the problem with this Danny, the Talmudic critic of Jewish wisdoms, ancient and recent? The answer begins, of course, with the way Danny often says what he says. However acute his perception of the blemishes of Judaism, his resentment at what he sees often makes his critique altogether too caustic. His distortions, too, make it difficult for the listener to separate out the true kernel contained in his observation from the useless husk. But, as I said earlier, these problems do not adequately explain the strength of the responses animated by Danny's critiques. Along with these problems, there are, I would argue, two other qualities that make his criticism so difficult to hear. First, Danny allows himself to say things that many a Jew knows to be true but is afraid to admit. It is painful to face parts of reality one has worked hard to suppress, and Danny forces the viewer to do so. Second, Danny, on the big, bright screen of the modern movie-house, does what he does in public. It is Danny the *public* questioner and critic who causes such a stir in the Jewish gut. And it is here, ironically, that Danny may stray farthest from Jewish tradition, ancient and modern. But this claim requires many words of clarification.

Jewish tradition is well known for its questioning and even critical character. One of its foundational stories represents Abraham challenging God to be just with the residents of Sodom and Gomorrah. "Will the judge of all the world not do justice?" he exclaims (Gen. 18:25). If there are but ten righteous residents in the cities, Abraham argues, God must save the cities on their account. God does not have the right to act arbitrarily, Abraham seems to assume, and he lets God know it.

The same tradition of critique carries forward into classical rabbinic culture. Perhaps the most striking expression of this critical voice is found in the Talmud's famous representations of the death of Rabbi Aqiba by the hands of the Romans in the early second century. In one of the Talmud's versions (tractate Menahot, p. 29b), the deceased Moses ascends to heaven to find God tying decorative crowns on the tops of letters in the Torah scroll. Moses inquires into the purpose of these crowns and is told that, many generations in the future, Rabbi Aqiba will use them as the basis for deriving laws. Moses asks to be transported into Aqiba's school in order to witness his interpretive skills and, finding himself impressed and even amazed, Moses questions God concerning Aqiba's future reward. God then transports Moses to the setting in which Aqiba's life ends. Moses is made to witness the flesh of Aqiba, who has been tortured and murdered by the Romans, being weighed out in the marketplace. How does Moses respond to this grisly scene? "This is Torah and this its reward?" he protests. God, in the story, is permitted to offer only a feeble response: "This is what it occurred to me to do."

Rooted in the historical reality of persecutions of Jews by the Romans during the revolt led by Bar Kochba (133-5 C.E.), this Talmudic story bears witness to the brutality of that experience. But the story's most remarkable element is the way it responds to that brutality: Moses, the giver of Torah, the great hero of rabbinic tradition, is made to articulate the ultimate question—how can God allow one who observes God's Torah to suffer so grievously and unjustly? In fact, it is difficult to imagine a more challenging theological question, whether in antiquity or today. Yet it is Moses, in this version of the story, or the Ministering Angels, in the Talmud's other version (tractate Berakhot, p. 61b), who expresses it. It is not the evil rebel who gives voice to this challenge, not the unbeliever who wonders how God can be passive in the face of such cruelty. It is the wisest, the most respected figure in the tradition—indeed, the true "Believer"—

who, as the Talmud understands it, will speak the truth and protest false pieties.

I think it is fair to say that both of these stories—the biblical challenge by Abraham and the Talmudic protest by Moses—are examples of the rebuke of God. In each case, the hero seems to enact the biblical command, "you shall surely rebuke your neighbor (Lev. 19:17)," in connection with God. The fact that the object of each rebuke is the divine covenantal partner does not remove this model from the human realm, though. It merely demonstrates how deeply the obligation to offer correction is embedded in the covenantal ideal. If it is appropriate to rebuke even God for perceived wrongs or injustices, how much more necessary is it to offer correction to human partners in the covenant of Israel.

But here is the rub. The command of Leviticus directs a person to offer private, personal rebuke to his neighbor. Indeed, the Talmud, emphasizing the difficulty of properly fulfilling this directive, cautions that one not attempt to rebuke another if he or she is unlikely to be able to "hear" it. Undoubtedly, correction offered in public is more difficult, if not impossible, to hear. Contrary to what we might assume, the Talmud's critical challenge of God's justice, spoken by Moses, is a "private" rebuke. How can this be so, given that it is expressed in what is, prima facie, a public document? In reality, the Talmud is an insider's work, accessible, until modernity, only to scholars who had undertaken long years of specialized study. "Private" here means inside, and there is no doubt that insiders might share questions and critiques that would be inappropriate if spoken in a more public domain. And even the Torah's rebuke, offered in the voice of Abraham, is less than public in the sense just defined. It is unimaginable that the Torah was meant, in its origins, to be recited beyond the circle of Israel. Besides, Abraham's complaint for justice in the story of Sodom and Gomorrah is more than offset by the silent, accepting Abraham of the "Akedah." It is the latter Abraham whose model echoed most powerfully in the traditional worlds of both Jews and Christians in later centuries.

So, when we return to Danny, whose critique is arguably the critique of a believer in the ancient model, we must ask whether his is a rebuke offered in a manner in which it might be heard. He is obviously not speaking in the company of insiders, as one Jew to his neighbor. He yells his critique mostly as an outsider, no matter how powerfully his emotions draw him back to the Jewish center. And his fictional voice is expressed by means of that most public of contemporary media—film. Can such a rebuke fulfill the ideal of Leviticus? Or is Danny's—and Bean's—the way of the Talmudic informer, who is hated for telling even the truth in a way that can be hurtful to his people?

Let me define the category of "informer" by relating an example from the midrash. In the midrash's version of the drama of Esther and Mordechai, the wicked Haman seeks to destroy the Jews by enticing them to participate in sin (if they sin, God will have to punish them). Haman persuades Mordechai to invite his Jewish subjects to an orgy and, despite Mordechai's attempt to dissuade them, many willingly attend. At the moment they begin to participate in sinful activity, Satan arises and speaks against them before God. Informing God of their sin, Satan succeeds in persuading God to destroy them (of course, this is not the end of the story).

The informer, in this story, is Satan. In other rabbinic stories, the informer might be the snake (from the Garden of Eden). Without exception, the informer is a hated or condemned figure, and what makes him hateful is his willingness to speak against Israel, often to foreign authorities (such as the Romans), in a way that brings them harm. This is so whether or not what he says against Israel is true.

The hatred of the informer in Jewish tradition and history was extreme. The rabbis instituted a prayer, to be recited three times daily, to curse the informer. The Talmud insists that informers will be punished in Hell for all generations, with no hope of a reprieve. In Europe in the Middle Ages—and particularly in Spain—the plague of informers was so profound that local Jewish courts sometimes condemned them to death, buying the cooperation of the authorities to carry out the court's verdict.

Why was the attitude toward informers so excessive? Obviously, because their actions potentially brought harm, whether economic or physical, to the Jewish community. During centuries when the well-being of Jews was repeatedly placed in jeopardy, the possible harm done by the imprudent speech of insiders could not be tolerated. When the consequences might be so grievous, the community understood itself to have the right—a right with which we will sympathize—to suppress the potentially damaging utterance.

So our question is, is Danny a rebuker, seeking to correct the wrongs he perceives as a sympathetic compatriot, or an informer, bringing potential harm to his former community by exposing their blemishes to the gaze of unsympathetic outsiders? Before responding too quickly—isn't the latter the *obvious* answer?—let us examine a contemporary analogy that may force us to reconsider.

Jewish organizations in the United States have repeatedly condemned the mainstream press for what they allege to be biased reporting concerning Israel. They commonly insist that Israel and her policies are represented critically and unfairly in the American media. The Jewish press, by contrast, will be described as fairer or more objective in its reporting. This is despite the fact that the American news media broadcast or publish a wide variety of views concerning events in the Middle East, whereas the American Jewish press prints a narrow range of acceptable opinions. Indeed, the Jewish press is characterized by a kind of "Israel-orthodoxy" that will almost always support "Israel's side" of any incident or dispute.

Notably, the habits of the American Jewish press are not replicated in Israel. Israeli newspapers are generally a wide-open affair, printing opinions from a broad range of perspectives. And, whether leaning to the right or to the left, they do not hesitate to express criticism—often biting criticism—of their government, its leaders, and their policies. I offer a few select recent examples:

During the recent Passover holiday (2001), Israeli Prime Minister Ariel Sharon offered lengthy interviews to the three leading Israeli papers. Sharon spoke of the recent conflict with the Palestinians, of the current state of Zionism, and of his own past. Subsequently, columnists in each of the papers criticized Sharon for being naïve or out of touch—for viewing the world of today through the lens of yesterday. The language they used to offer their critique was sometimes less than respectful. But this is typical of Israeli political rhetoric, in the newspapers as much as in the street.

On the occasion of Israel's Independence Day, one columnist wrote at length of Israel's failure to respect the needs and rights of her Arab citizens in connection with the public commemoration. For the Arabs, Israel's Independence Day is a day of bitter memories— memories that find no legitimate public expression. Where, the writer asked, are the monuments to the hundreds of Arab towns and villages inside the Green Line that were destroyed during the War of Independence? Why is the memory of these villages suppressed or erased in official Israeli policy, for Jewish and Arab citizens of the state alike? This was a biting, bitter op-ed piece, one that surely upset many readers. But, in the Israeli press, it had its place.

A more recent column questioned the justice of Israeli policies in the West Bank during the protracted intifada, policies that protect the right of relatively few Jewish settlers to move about freely while restricting or confining the mobility of hundreds of thousands of Palestinians. Why, the author wondered, must Israel expend its resources, and oppress and alienate the local population, to protect settlers whose right many Israelis oppose in the first place? Whatever wrongs might be committed by Palestinian militants cannot erase the wrong promulgated by this Israeli military policy, or so the columnist argued.

I cannot remember the last time I saw opinions like these expressed in the American Jewish press. Indeed, I think it is fair to say that they would be unprintable. One frequent contributor to the Jewish press recently told me that he is unable to express his true opinions concerning the "situation" in Israel and the West Bank for fear that he would jeopardize his career.

But how can we explain this dichotomy between the Israeli and American-Jewish press? Why will one community permit the out-spoken expression of critique and dissent when the other will not? A sympathetic explanation would reference the "inside-outside" distinction adumbrated above. The Israeli press is an "inside" press. In the Israeli papers (as well as other media), Israelis speak to Israelis. In those papers, therefore, commentators may feel free to express their opinions—whatever those opinions might be—as openly as they like, for there is no fear of doing harm when the audience is one's brothers and sisters. But the American Jewish press is, in some sense, an "out-side" organ, for it represents Israel (as well as the Jewish community) before the American populace at large. Expressed in American Jewish papers, certain views might do harm, for critical comments could be (mis)interpreted as evidence of absence of support for Israel. So, the argument would go, it is better to exclude critical opinions from the Anglo-Jewish press, even at the expense of community self-censorship.

Whatever the logic of this distinction, it is impossible to sustain in a world where the critical Israeli op-ed, in English, is only as far away as the click of a mouse. With information technologies being what they are, there is no longer a real difference between "inside" and "outside." All expression for the record is "outside"; it is all "public" in the widest sense of the word. What is written one day for the Israeli paper can be picked up the next day by the *New York Times* or the *Washington Post*. And it often is. Furthermore, opinion writers in Israel are well aware of this fact. Their judgment is that there is no need to suppress critical opinions, even when the "audience" is the world.

Moreover, even in the absence of current electronic technologies, it is impossible to imagine an "inside" and "outside" when speaking of Israel-related opinion. Israel operates on the world stage. Her actions and policies are debated in the public forum. She has no secrets because, in this world, there would be no way to keep a "secret" secret for very long.

In a world such as this, the very distinction between "inside" and "outside" is pernicious, and the belief that what one says among insiders will not be heard among outsiders simply naïve. In reality, we have no choice but to speak with the recognition that, whatever we say, anyone may listen. For this reason, it is essential that any expression be defensible before the scrutiny of the broadest possible audience. Israeli opinion-makers understand this, and they therefore allow themselves to speak their mind, whoever might hear. Do I speak the truth as I understand it?—this is the question each must ask. In contrast, the American Jewish press, which is afraid of the scrutiny of the outsider, limits expression and disallows dissent. And, for this reason, it is scorned by knowledgeable insiders.

The Jewish community, like Israel—like *all* communities—lives today in the public square. Its actions and opinions are viewed and scrutinized by all who care to look. The traditional Jewish distinction between the rebuker and the informer may, therefore, no longer be sustained. If it is impossible to speak amongst insiders alone, it is necessary to speak honestly in the presence of all. Rebuke, like all sacred obligations, is performed in the open. Arguably, the nature of rebuke must therefore change. But it would be a mistake to conclude that the public nature of the act requires that it be softened, the sharpness of the criticism blunted. Remember: Any compromise with conscience will be a *public* compromise. A partial rebuke will be seen for what it is, that is, only a half-truth. If the obligation to rebuke changes in the contemporary setting, it can be only in the direction of "full disclosure." The rebuke must be spoken as honestly as possible. This is so because, living together in a vast glass house, there will be no "sin" that will not be seen.

But, though a rebuke must be expressed honestly, it must still be offered in a manner in which it might be heard. And here, there is admittedly doubt whether Danny's—or shall we say Bean's—critique succeeds. Danny's violence, both physical and verbal, makes him a problematic messenger for rebuke. Moreover, the distortions that are often the vehicle for his messages make it difficult to hear what is right in what he says; some viewers will simply be too consumed in trying to correct his distortions. These problematic qualities, it may be argued, are in the service of dramatic characterization. Danny does successfully demand that we sit up and take notice, and, we must admit, the rebuker to whom we pay no attention is no rebuker at all. But is this justification enough to mitigate the extremism and brutality that will make some viewers so uncomfortable? Only the individual viewer can answer for him or herself.

My answer to this question? An unhesitating yes. It seems to me that the voice of *The Believer* is the voice of one who loves Jewish tradition but hates its flaws. And both are spoken with total honesty, at least as the rebuker understands it. In his view, the Torah is mysterious and sacred, its discipline one that provides direction and comfort. But the same Torah is also a repository of sometimes arbitrary and even cruel laws, and its discipline more than once seems an exercise of divine power for its own sake. Can there be any denying the wisdom of this insight?

Does the bile of the messenger diminish the profundity of his message? For me, the answer is no. First, because his resentment and outrage are real, if exaggerated. Who cannot feel resentment at the injustices of this, as of any, tradition? Who will deny the outrage of historical victimhood transformed into cultural value? Second, because for most people—and I include myself in this category—it is difficult to articulate critiques of a tradition one loves, and where I might vacillate, Danny does not hesitate. In the end, I believe, critiques are better expressed than not expressed. Finally, because I am a Jew who is committed to the tradition of my people, I too must stand among the rebuked. And I think that I am better able to hear the rebuke because it is, by virtue of its dramatic context, oblique and not direct.

The Believer offers a model for what might be described as a postmodern rebuke. As we have noted, in the age of (potentially) universal public access to information, no rebuke, however culturally specific, can be truly private. Being public, perhaps it is wisest that rebuke be expressed indirectly, in the heightened reality of film rather than in the pious banality of a sermon. Because it is refracted through the artistic medium, the one who cannot hear it will not. He or she will turn aside or dismiss it as absurd. Still, in the distorted voice of dramatic exaggeration, a truer critique might well reside, and that critique will be heard by the one who is willing to listen. *The Believer* is an experiment in such postmodern rebuke and, whether successful as rebuke or not, its intuition is brilliant.

Jewish Self-Hatred (I)
and
The Believer (II)

Sander L. Gilman

I

S elf-criticism" had, for German Jews, a strongly positive conno-
tation well into the 1880s. Moritz Lazarus could speak pridefully
of the Jews as the classical people of "self-criticism" in his pamphlet *What Is National?* And Emanuel Schreiber, the rabbi of the
Bonn Jewish community, in 1881 published an entire book on the
"self-criticism of the Jews," in which this quality is glorified and
exemplified by his own attack on the neo-Orthodox Breslau Rab-
binical Seminary. His attack, he argues, should not be taken as "self
hatred" because 1) it is valid and 2) he is not condemning all Jews, just
a subset. It is only with the increase in virulent public anti-Semitism,
with its concomitant identification among German Jews with the
Eastern Jew as an idealized image of the "good Jew," that the concept
of "self-criticism" is replaced by the pathology of "self-hatred," an illness attributed to Jews. Jews had been long the subject of medical
discourse, first as healer and then as part of that group most at risk
from disease, reaching back into the Middle Ages. The merging of
the image of the self-critical Jew with that of the mad Jew produced,
in the final decades of the nineteenth century, the image of the self-
hating Jew as art of the rhetoric of race. A half-century after the
French Revolution, within the confines of the Parisian Anthropological Society, the question of specifically Jewish tendencies toward illness, their form and frequency, was raised again. It was at the time of
the most visible demands of French Jewry for a share in the power of
the bourgeoisie, who had attempted to exclude them in the Third

Republic. In the *Bulletin* of the Anthropological Society, M. Boudin commented in a letter from Vichy concerning "idiocy and mental illness among German Jews" based on German census statistics. The focus of this short paper was on the much higher frequency of psychopathologies among Jews in Germany than among Catholics or Protestants in the same population. For example, in Bavaria one mentally ill individual was found for a population of 908 Catholics and 967 Protestants but for only 514 Jews. This led Boudin to observe that psychopathologies are "twice as frequent among the Jewish population as among the German population." Boudin attributed this to "the frequency of marriage between blood relatives." Statistics as a means of quantifying insanity as a sign of Otherness had been used following the 1840 American census. In the interpretation of that data, the antiabolitionist forces, headed by John C. Calhoun, had argued that blacks suffered more frequently from mental illness when free than when enslaved; thus, freedom promoted psychopathology. For Boudin, inbreeding, the exclusivity of the Jews, was the pseudoscientific origin of the Jews' tendency to psychopathology. The contemporary demand for legal equality was translated into its antithesis, the desire for psychopathology. Boudin also focused on the problem in Germany, rather than in France, distancing it even more. For the French, the German Jew became the Other. Boudin concluded his paper with a critique of the view that the etiology of psychopathology among the Jews could be traced to their "cosmopolitanism." The idea that the Jew is associated with modern civilization and the decadence of city life was introduced here, if only to be rebutted. What for LaFontaine had been a general predisposition to illness had become by the mid-nineteenth century a predisposition for mental illness. The Jews were seen as covertly ill in a manner that provided observers with proof of their own emotional and intellectual superiority.

The statistics brought by nineteenth- (and indeed twentieth-) century writers on the topic of the mental instability of the Jews do not, of course, reflect any specific predisposition of the European Jewish community for mental illness. Indeed, this view has recently been labeled one of the "misconceptions" about the genetic disorders that befall the Jews. The statistics, cited over and over by mental health practitioners during this period, most probably reflect the higher incidence of hospitalization of Jews for mental illness owing to their concentration in urban areas, which, unlike rural areas, were not as conducive to the presence of the mentally ill within society. Also, urban Jews had developed a better network for the identification and treatment of illness, including mental illness. The sense of community, coupled with the impression that the mentally ill were unable to function within urban society, may have led to more frequent hospitalization and thus to the higher statistical incidence of psychopathology among the Jews.

By the 1880s the linkage of the Jew with psychopathology was a given in anthropological circles. In the Parisian Anthropological Society the Prussian census of 1880 was the point of departure for an even more detailed debate on the psychopathologies of the Jews. Again statistics were used to stress the greater occurrence of mental illness among the Jews. The comments on the etiology of mental illness are more diffuse. M. Zabrowski laid it at the feet of the ecstatic preoccupation with mysticism and the supernatural, a clear reference to the Eastern Jews, whose presence was being felt even more in Paris following the assassination of Alexander II in 1881 and the resulting forced immigration. He and M. Sanson also stressed the curative role of agricultural employment and the absence of Jews in this field. The "cosmopolitanism" of the Jews, the pressure of the fields in which they were occupied, formed part of the reason for him. But M. Blanchard simply stated that "hysteria and neurasthenia are more frequent among the Jewish race than all other races." Thus it was no longer simply mental illness, itself a delimitation of LaFontaine's more general view of the Jewish predisposition for illness, but rather "hysteria and neurasthenia" that were typical of the Jew. The source, according to M. Sanson, was endogamous marriage.

The view that all Jews were especially prone to hysteria and neurasthenia through inbred weakening of the nervous system appeared in canonical form in Jean Martin Charcot's *Tuesday Lesson* for October 23, 1888. Charcot, Freud's teacher, described "a case of hysterical dysnie. I already mentioned that his twenty-year-old patient is a Jewess. I will use this occasion to stress that nervous illnesses of all types are innumerably more frequent among Jews than among other groups." Charcot attributed this fact to inbreeding.

By 1890 Charcot's view had become a commonplace in European psychiatry. Standard German textbooks of psychiatry such as those by Schule, Kraeplin, Kirchhoff and Krafft-Ebing cited Charcot. For Krafft-Ebing the "anthropological" cause of the greater incidence of insanity among the Jews is their endogamous marriages which he, as a liberal, compares to the degeneracy found in the inbred upper class. But it is mysticism, as in the image of the Eastern Jew, that he contrasts with the rationality of the Western religion. The result of this stress of inbreeding and mysticism is to focus on the exclusivity of the Jews. The form of this insanity has sexual implications:

> Very often, excessive religious inclination is itself a symptom of an originally abnormal character of actual disease, and, not infrequently, concealed under a veil of religious enthusiasm there is abnormally intensified sensuality and sexual excitement that lead to sexual errors that are of etiological significance.

It is in the description of neurasthenia in Krafft-Ebing's study of the illness that the image of the Jewish man is to be found. He is "an over-achiever in the arena of commerce or politics" who "reads reports, business correspondence, stock market notations during meals, for whom 'time is money.'" The association of the Jew with the "American illness," through the use of the English phrase "time is money," presents the cosmopolitan Jew as the quintessential American. This conflation of two personifications of Otherness underlines the political implications of seeing in the "cosmopolitanism" of the Jews, in their function in the modern city, the source, on one level, of their neurasthenia. Yet this integration of the Jews into the negative image of modern civilization is contradicted by the view of the exclusivity of the Jews in their sexual isolation from Western society.

The image of the neurasthenic as Jew is not found as widely within Krafft-Ebing's text, however (even though he elsewhere in the same text stresses the special proclivity of the Jew for neurasthenia). Rather, this analogy of the Jews is written from the Jewish point of view. The quote was used in Martin Engländer's essay *The Evident Most Frequent Appearances of Illness in the Jewish Race* (1902). Engländer was one of the early Viennese supporters of Herzl and the Zionist movement. He discussed the cultural predisposition of the Jews to neurasthenia as a result of the "over-exertion and exhaustion of the brain...among Jews as opposed to the non-Jewish population." "The struggle, haste and drive, the hunt for happiness" have caused a "reaction in their central nervous system." Neurasthenia is the result of the Jewish brain's inability to compete after "a two-thousand-year Diaspora" and "a struggle for mere existence up to emancipation." Engländer thus attempted to dismiss the etiology of neurasthenia as a result of inbreeding, citing the Americans as an example of a "race" in which neurasthenia predominates and in which exogamous marriages are common. The cause of the Jews' illnesses is their confinement in the city, the source of all degeneracy; the cure is "land, air, light."

Engländer's views are not idiosyncratic. For him the madness of the Jews is a direct result of the Jews' political and social position in the West. Cesare Lombroso, whose name is linked with the concept of "degeneration" which he helped forge, was also a Jew. After authoring a number of studies on the degeneracy of the prostitute and the criminal, Lombroso was confronted with the charge that Jews, too, were a degenerate subclass of human being, a class determined by their biology. Lombroso's answer to this charge, *Anti-Semitism and the Jews in the Light of Modern Science* (1893), attempted to counter the use of medical or pseudoscientific discourse to characterize the nature of the Jew. But Lombroso also accepted the basic view that the Jew was more highly prone to specific forms of mental illness. He quotes Charcot to this effect, but, like Engländer, he sees the reason for this tendency not in the physical nature of the Jew but in the "residual effect of persecution." Both Engländer and Lombroso accepted the view that some type of degenerative process, leading to the predominance of specific forms of mental illness, exists among all Jews. The only difference from non-Jewish savants that they saw was the cause of this process. In rejecting the charge of inbreeding, Jews such as Engländer and Lombroso also rejected the implications that they indulge in primitive sexual practices that violate a basic human taboo against incest. The confusion of endogamous marriage with incestuous inbreeding was a result both of the level of late-nineteenth-century science and of the desire of this scientific discourse to have categories with which to label the explicit nature of the Other. The Jews are thus mentally ill, they manifest this illness in the forms of hysteria and neurasthenia, and the cause is their sexual practice or their mystical religion or their role as carriers of Western cosmopolitanism.

It is in this context that Max Nordau's often cited call for the Jews to become "muscle Jews," published in 1900, must be read. German nationalism through the code of *mens sana in corpore sano* is evident. But, of course, this earlier call by the father of German nationalism, *Turnvater* Jahn, had been heavily overladen with anti-Semitic rhetoric. Nordau's call is yet another attempt from within the Jewish community to co-opt the underlying premises of anti-Semitic rhetoric and use its strong political message for their own ends. Nordau's call for a "new muscle Jew" is based on the degeneration of the Jew "in the narrow confines of the ghetto." But not only the Jews' muscles but also their minds have atrophied in the ghetto. Implicit in Nordau's call is the equation of the "old Jews" and their attitude toward life. Zionism demands that the new muscle Jew have a healthy body and a healthy mind. Thus he condemns his critics as having not only weak bodies but weak minds! This charge must be read within the inner circles of the Zionist movement in which (as has been seen) the opponents of Zionism are viewed as merely Jews possessing all of the qualities ascribed to them (including madness) by the anti-Semites.

Neurasthenia, the American disease, the disease of modern life, is also the disease of the Jews, modern people incarnate. Degeneration was the result of sexuality and was symptomized by deviant sexuality. If the best authorities were to be believed, and at least in Germany the best authorities argued that inbreeding was the cause of the neurasthenia of the Jews, there is more than a slight implication of incest. Indeed, Engländer expressly defends the Jews against the charge of "racial inbreeding" while condemning the provisions of Mosaic law that permit marriage between uncle and niece. He thus gives evidence to the implicit charge that runs through all the literature on the insanity of the Jews; that they are themselves the cause of their own downfall through their perverse sexuality and that their degeneracy is the outward sign of their fall from grace. The sexuality of the Other is always threatening. With the implicit charge of incest, one of the ultimate cultural taboos of nineteenth-century thought is evoked. Inbreeding is incestuous and is a sign of the "primitive" nature of the Jews, of their existence outside the bounds of acceptable, Western sexual practice.

The discourse of decadent civilization, of the city, is inexorably linked with the sexual exclusivity of the Jew. Nowhere is this linkage made more evident than in Thomas Mann's novella *The Blood of the Walsungen* (1905). This tale of brother-sister incest ends, at least in the first version, with an emphasis on the sexual exclusivity of the Jew. The brother has just consummated his relationship with his sister, and she ponders the fate of her German fiancé. Mann concludes the unpublished first edition with two Yiddishisms, a sign of the damaged, sexualized discourse of the siblings. Mann's father-in-law,

Alfred Pringsheim, so objected to the inclusion of Yiddishisms ("We robbed [beganeft] the non-Jew [goy]") as a sign of the siblings' ethnic identity that Mann suppressed the planned publication of the story. The novella, which Mann re-edited in 1921 to eliminate the Yiddishisms, echoed the sense of the corruption of both "modern life" as typified by the Wagner cult and the Jews. The Jews, through their lack of redemption, are morally weak, and this manifests itself in the most primitive manner, through incest. Indeed, Adolf Hitler, never the most original of thinkers, simply summarized "Jewish religious doctrine" as "prescriptions for keeping the blood of Jewry pure." The view that within the Jews' sexuality is hidden the wellspring of their own degeneration haunts the overtly sexual imagery of anti-Semitic writings from the end of the nineteenth century. The Jew, the most visible Other in late-nineteenth-century Europe, is also the bearer of the most devastating sexual stigma, incest.

Even those Jews who accepted the idea that the Jew was predisposed to some form of mental illness, a concept articulated in the rhetoric of racial science, could not accept it as applied to themselves. Rather, they projected the idea of an innate tendency to psychopathology onto other groups of Jews, the "bad" Jews, with whom they refused to identify. Parallel to the invention of the Eastern Jew as the image of the ideal Jew, separate from the corruption of all Western traditions, there arises the image of the self-hating Jew as the necessary product of this Western tradition. In 1904 Fritz Wittels continued the argument of writers such as Conrad Alberti that those Jews who accept the value systems of German society are condemned to self-hatred. In his pamphlet *The Baptized Jew* he adopts the entire *topos* of the hidden language of the Jews as presented in the rhetoric of science. Baptized Jews are, for Wittles, simply Jews who have "perjured themselves for base reasons"; they are lying Jews. These Jews have the capacity to become "anti-Semitic" Jews. We have already seen that Karl Kraus used the concept of "Jewish anti-Semitism" in speaking of the Zionists. He postulated his perception of a "correct" Jewish identity as the basis for any definition of the "good" Jew and saw in Herzl and the Zionists the antithesis: they were Jews who hated other Jews and, by definition, themselves. For Fritz Wittels, the ultimate form of the baptized Jew is the Jew who hates his or her own race. Wittels, a follower and biographer of Freud, began to outline in his pamphlet the psychosis of self-hatred.

Some saw self-hatred as a necessary attribute of the "good" Jew.

Weininger uses a primitive understanding of the concept of projection in describing the process of self-hatred:

> Thus the fact this explained that the bitterest anti-Semites are to be found amongst the Jews themselves. For only the quite Jewish Jews, like the completely Aryan Aryans, are not at all anti-Semitically disposed; among the remainder only the commoner natures are actively anti-Semitic and pass sentence on others without having once sat in judgment on themselves in these matters; and very few exercise their anti-Semitism first on themselves. This one thing, however, remains nonetheless certain; whoever detests the Jewish disposition detests it first of all in himself; that he should persecute it in others is merely his endeavor to separate himself from Jewishness; he strives to shake it off and to localize it in his fellow-creatures, and so for a moment to dream himself free of it. Hatred, like love, is a projected phenomenon; that person alone is hated who reminds one unpleasantly of oneself.

Weininger's awareness of projection as a psychological mechanism is but another adaptation of the rhetoric of science, here the science of psychology, to the psychopathology of the Jew. Both Wittels the psychoanalyst and Weininger the philosopher employ the model of the self-hater as one who embodies all of the essential negative qualities ascribed to the Jew. Weininger and Wittels have created a subclass for the psychology of the Jew that points toward self-hatred as the marker of the Jew most closely identifying with the double bind inherent in Western culture. This "double bind" is at the crux of the problem of self-hatred. As an assimilated or secular Jew, in order to be a "full" member of a society that believes in the inherent inferiority of the Jews, one needs to believe in one's own inferiority. This is virtually impossible (except in the model of self-destructive masochism) and thus one projects this sense of difference on to "other" Jews.

Both Wittels and Weininger see the self-hating Jew as the apogee (or nadir) of this identification. But both present this as a problem in the psychology of race. This shift in the rhetoric of science, or at least the continuation of the biology of race into a biological psychology of race, represents the very beginnings of an explanatory model of self-hatred rooted in a dynamic psychology.

With the gradual replacement during the opening decades of the twentieth century of the biologically determined model for psychopathology with that of a psychodynamically oriented one, one would have expected the image of the madness of the Jew to have vanished. With Freud's reorientation of psychopathology, any particularistic attribution of specific patterns of mental disease to any group, especially on the basis of a presumed group-specific sexual aberration, should have been impossible. But Freud's views of the universal patterns of human sexuality, especially in regard to fantasies of incest, could not destroy the image of the Jew as predisposed to mental illness. This view continued, not only in the theoretical writings of Wittels and Weininger, but in the clinic where the most radical rethinking of the etiology of mental illness was being undertaken.

In Eugen Bleuler's Burghölzli, the clinic in which Freud's dynamic psychopathology was being applied in a hospital setting, Rafael Becker, a young Jewish doctor, was given the assignment of comparing Jewish and non-Jewish patients to determine whether the work done by earlier investigators could be validated with the psychoanalytic approach. Becker first presented his findings before a Zionist organization in Zurich during March 1919. He began with the statistics upon which everyone had based their assumptions and thus predetermined his own findings. The Jews do indeed suffer from a more frequent rate of mental illness than the non-Jewish population, but not because of inbreeding. Indeed, inbreeding has led to the Jews' becoming less frequently infected by certain illnesses, such as smallpox and cholera, since they "acquire immunizing force through inbreeding and the purity of the race." Becker also denies that there is any specific "psychosis judäica," any specific form of mental illness that affects only the Jews, any more than there are any specific anthropological signs that determine the inferiority of the Jews. Mental illness for Becker (as for Bleuer) was not brain illness but psychic illness. Becker dismisses the increase in luetic infections and their results, as well as senile dementia, among the Jews as merely social artifacts; these are the result of alteration in society in general—the spread of syphilis in the former case and the increased life expectancy provided by better social conditions in the latter.

Becker denies any specific increase in mental illness because of a special proclivity of the Jews but sees in the increase in the rate of other forms of psychopathology the direct result of the acculturation of Western Jews. Becker notes that even though Jews in earlier times suffered more greatly from oppression, their strong faith preserved their sanity. Only with the decline in Jewish identity in the nineteenth century has there been an increase in mental illness. Becker picks up a thread in late-nineteenth-century anti-assimilationist Jewish thought that places the roots for the moral decline of the Jew at the doorstep of Jewish emancipation and acculturation. He introduces Alfred Adler's newly coined concept of "inferiority" to give a dynamic dimension to his assumption that Jews are more frequently driven into madness than their non-Jewish persecutors. It is the "assimilated Jew" who is diseased, self-hating and thus self-destructive.

Becker outlines the steps in the etiology of Jewish psychopathology. He denies any role to degeneration caused by inbreeding. He observes that because Jews are forbidden *de facto* the practice of certain occupations, many Jews marry very late. As a result, they have fewer and fewer children. (This is a substantial change from the charge made in the eighteenth century that the Jews' illnesses came from their early marriages and their large number of children!) As a result, the normal sexual development of the Jew is stunted because of the lack of an appropriate sexual outlet. Becker provided his audience with a solution that they would immediately have accepted as correct. He sees an alteration of the social structure that caused such illnesses as the appropriate "therapy." Provide appropriate occupations, resolve the sense of inferiority that results from being unable to enter the profession that one desires, and earlier marriages will occur, which will remove the direct cause of the psychopathologies. In the meantime, Jews can avoid the causes of overstimulation of sexuality by avoiding alcohol and sharp spices ("so beloved in the Jewish cuisine") and by exercising, following Nordau's prescription. This was Becker's presentation before a Jewish lay audience in 1918; the next year he published the results of his scholarly researches in the Burghölzli, which repeat many of his earlier views. He provides a case study of the inferiority complex of one of his patients, a thirty-eight-year-old merchant. The case study provides Becker with an illness that he now sees as the result of the position of the Jew in Western society. Not a "psychosis judäica" but rather, using the new rhetoric of psychoanalysis, "the Jewish complex." The Jewish complex in this patient, illustrated by long passages form the patient's own biographical account, is marked by the sense of inferiority brought about by his treatment in society from the age of four, when "at the market day in Altstätten I alone of all the children was mocked...I felt the humiliation that the Jew as a human being must feel in society.". Becker's patient continues to describe his life in terms of the social inferiority that he perceived as a Jewish child in a Christian world. Even though Becker records a fairly detailed description of the patient's sexual life, he sees in all of the anomalies of his sexuality only the product of the social inequality that led to his sense of inferiority. Thus Becker is able to avoid any relationship between the inborn sexual perversities ascribed to the Jew and his psychosis.

The theme of Jewish self-hatred reappears in the language of psychoanalysis in 1923 when Josef Prager writes an essay for Martin Buber's *The New Jew* entitled "Repression and Breakthrough in the Jewish Soul." Seeing Freud as an essentially Jewish thinker, Prager attempts to use the concept of repression as a tool for understanding the shaping of the "Jewish soul." He sees the conflict as existing between the norms of society and the ability of the Jew to adapt to them. When the society attaches negative evaluation to being Jewish, Jews who desire to be assimilated must repress these attributes, and in repressing them, they come to have a centrality for them. Now Prager sees this repression as being a quality of the drive for assimilation, and he sees in the articulation of one's Jewishness the first step to a "healing of the sick Jewish soul." Prager picks up the thread of a specific Jewish illness, an illness of the Jewish soul in Western society, which is "self-hatred." It is not the Eastern Jew but rather Westernized Jew who is sick, and the illness is one of the psyche. Here the process of projection is complete. Articulated through the new "Jewish" language of psychoanalysis (the Viennese answer to Hebrew as a cultural language), Prager's argument implicitly presents the Eastern Jew as one free of such ills.

In 1924, E. J. Lesser provides another case study: Karl Marx as self-hater. But Lesser hits on a new tack, seeing in Marx's self-hatred his Jewishness. Marx's language is that of the Jew in that he uses the *pilpul* in his argument. His Jewish identity even appears when he is damning the Jews. No matter what he undertakes, he remains the "full-blooded Jew." What is interesting is that other discussions of Marx's self-hatred in this period came to the same conclusion. They return to Buber's model of a conflict between Jewish identity and Western civilization to explain the aberration of self-hatred. Self-hatred is thus the denial of the essential Jew within; it is the dialectical process undertaken within the psyche. The essential Jew in conflict with the values of the West produces the self-hater, that individual who typifies the Jew in the West.

With the rise of the Nazis, the image of the "self-hating" Jew, the self-critical Jew, became a touchstone for the political anti-Semites. Robert Weltsch, in an editorial in the *Jewish Panorama* of May 5, 1933, still called for the need for "self-criticism, in spite of everything." While rejecting the type of biologically defined self-hatred exemplified by Weininger, as well as German Jewish critical overcompensation, he called for an introspective evaluation of Jewish identity. He sees the striving for assimilation as an illness that led to these forms of self-hatred. The Jew must have a "Jewish national sense," which must arise through "self-criticism." Weltsch's observations rely on a dichotomy between healthy self-criticism and diseased self-hatred. Healthy are those who reject their acculturated identities and see themselves primarily as Jews; diseased are those who remain mired within the corruption of a primarily German identity. Again it is the label of the Other, here the acculturated German, as self-hating and thus diseased that creates categories of the acceptable and the unacceptable Jews. Weltsch's Zionist orientation sees the "new Jew" as consciously rejecting the model of identity that predominated among German Jews during the late nineteenth and early twentieth centuries. His glorification of a separatist Jewish identity is parallel to the stress on national identities present throughout Europe. Just as the Nazis claimed that being consciously German was "healthy" and being Jewish was "diseased" (a metaphor that dominates Hitler's *Mein Kampf*, so, too, it was necessary for Jewish political ideologists to distinguish between "healthy" and "corrupt" Jewish identities. What is evident is that their own sense of self provided the model for the "healthy" Jew; that which they rejected, the model for the "ill" Jew.

The German model for the formation of a "healthy" Jewish identity had some influence on the other side of the Atlantic. Given the great prestige of German medical science in the United States, it is of little wonder that the American medical establishment, or at least American Jewish psychiatrists, took interest in the psychopathology of self-hatred. In 1920 A. Myerson, at the Boston State Hospital, attributed the psychopathology of the Jew to "social" rather than "biological" heredity. Like Becker, he sees in the Jews' isolation from appropriate forms of work one of the major sources for their psychopathology. Myerson also sees in the rejection by the Jews of "sports and play" one of the sources of the illness of the Jew. Again following Norday's image of the "muscle Jew," here redefined as the "all-American athlete," Myerson provides yet another theoretical restatement of this myth:

Sports and play...form an incomparable avenue of discharge for nervous tension. They breed confidence in oneself. Being [extensor] in their character, they allow for the rise of pride and courage. Circumstances excluded the Jew from their wholesome influence, and the children of the race grew up to be very serious, very earnest, too early devoted to mature efforts, excessively cerebral in their activities, and not sufficiently strenuous physically. *In other words, the Jew, through his restrictions, was cheated out of childhood.*

Myerson, like Becker, needs to localize the baneful influence on the Jews outside of the Jews themselves. He locates it in another society, Eastern Europe, not America, with its reevaluation of older, foreign values. Indeed, the very fact that a large number of Eastern European Jews were manual laborers, under the most primitive conditions, relegates his condemnation of the image of the inactive Jewish child into the world of myth. For Myerson, the "bad" Jew as sick Jew resides in the East, is the Eastern Jew, the most evident representative of the stereotype of the Jew in post–First World War America.

The polemic attached to the idea of self-hatred as the pathological underpinning of the "bad" Jew continued in the United States throughout the mid-twentieth century. In Kurt Lewin's 1941 essay on Jewish self-hatred, Theodor Lessing's thesis of the innate psychosis of assimilated Jews trying to become "real" Germans (in his book of case studies of Jewish self-hatred of 1930) was examined within a social psychological model. Lewin, until 1932 professor of psychology at the University of Berlin and then the leading exponent of the study of group dynamics in the United States, was the major link between German concepts of self-hatred and American analysis of Jewish anti-Semitism. Lewin recognized, at least superficially, the false antithesis between the "bad" Eastern Jew and the "good" Western Jew in the German Jews' paradigm for the projection of their self-hatred. However, Lewin wishes to shift the discourse from one that sees self-hatred as an individual problem of adaptation, as in Lessing, to one of group dynamics. It is not the individual's need to compensate but rather the response of the group that is the source of self-hatred. Lewin believes that he is abandoning the labeling of the Jew as ill; instead, he is extending the idea, as in the older model, from a limited (though representative) number of Jews to the entire category. "In fact, neurotic trends in Jews are frequently the result of their lack of adjustment to just such group problems." Neurosis is the result, not of inbreeding, but of group dynamics. It is, however, not only the privileged group's pressure on the minority that induces this sense of inferiority for Lewin; if this were the case, would self-hatred not manifest itself among such groups such as American Catholics? Assuming that this statement is empirically valid, Lewin seeks the etiology of self-hatred and finds it in those "Jewish" institutions associated with the Eastern Jew:

> To build up such a feeling of group belongingness on the basis of active responsibility for the fellow Jew should be one of the outstanding policies of Jewish education. That does not mean that we can create in our children a feeling of belongingness by *forcing* them to go to Sunday school or *Heder*. Such a procedure means the establishment in early childhood of the same pattern of enforced group belongingness which is characteristic of the psychological situation for the negative chauvinists and it is sure to create in the long run exactly this attitude. Too many young Jews are driven away by too much *Heder*.

Lewin contrasts the German ideal of *Bildung*, education, with the institutional structures in traditional Judaism that have been viewed since the Enlightenment as antithetical to true education. Indeed, when G. E. Lessing's quintessential Jew Nathan the Wise educates his adopted daughter Recha, he turns her out so that she may learn from nature instead of educating her within "Jewish" structures such as the *Heder*, or Hebrew school. Lewin's insights about the nature of group dynamics still revolve about the hidden agenda of the nature of sub-groups of Jews. Under the mask of the "self-hating" Western Jew still lurk presuppositions about the mythic Eastern Jew, presuppositions present within American Jewry just as they are within German Jewry. The sick Jew is the Eastern Jew.

In 1939 the Austrian psychologist Bruno Bettelheim was released from Buchenwald and emigrated to the United States. Based in Chicago, Bettelheim began to write a series of essays on his experiences in the concentration camps. One of these essays, incorporated in 1960 in his wide-reaching study of the Jewish response to the Holocaust, *The Informed Heart*, was a study entitled "The Dynamism of

Anti-Semitism in Gentile and Jew." Bettelheim sharpened the category of Jewish self-hatred in this essay and provided an elaborate model of self-hatred as the rationale for the inability of Jews to survive the camps. In contrast to Lewin, he locates the source of self-hatred in the assimilated Jew. He sees the loss of autonomy in the camps as parallel to the overall loss of autonomy in modern society, indeed as the reason for the fragmenting of personality within the camps. The Jews depend on the values of the society—on rank, position, status—to define themselves. When these are removed, when they are reduced to the level of the beast in their own eyes, their identities are destroyed. This is the red thread that is present in Buber and in Weininger: that the Jews in the West have no center, that they have replaced it (if indeed it ever existed) with the outward trappings of Western society, articulated in the political or economic discourse of the West. Bettelheim analyzes the reactions of the Jews, the "adaptive mechanisms" that they used to cope in the camps, as "neurotic or psychotic mechanisms," had they been manifested outside of the camps.

The Western Jews' actions are "insane" because they are in response to an "insane" world. The Jews have no center; they are insane. These responses internalize the anti-Semitic image of the Jew and they project it onto another subset of Jews, the Jews in the camps. Indeed, Bettelheim's initial "speculation[s] on the extermination camp" provide a five-point list of factors that "explain" the "docile acceptance of the situation in the camp." First, the prisoners are aware of the "tenuous" nature of their psychological "emergency measures"; second, they lose "libidinal energy" in maintaining their "fictions"; third, they identify with the enemy, which provides them with "gratification in being overpowered by the enemy"; fourth, they perceive the world as a psychotic delusion that can be maintained only by being passive and avoiding any direct confrontation with reality; fifth, in identifying with the "enemy" "they were able to 'destroy' delusionally their enemy by their own death." This pattern is, of course, the pattern of self-hatred developed within the rhetoric of the psychology of race during the early twentieth century. Self-haters know that their own self-hatred is but a coping device, they focus all of their energy in maintaining this device, they identify with the rhetoric of anti-Semitism, they use this rhetoric as a means of avoiding any confrontation with the reality of anti-Semitism in the streets, and finally, they so identify with the anti-Semite that they must end in suicide or madness.

The power of Lewin's and Bettelheim's contradictory models dominated the understanding of self-hatred following the war. The self-hating Jew is the "mad" Jew, and this Jew is the antithesis of the self-definition of the observer. In a 1951 dissertation entitled "Identification with the Aggressor," Irving Sarnoff attempted to document this type of identification through the use of standardized tests. Drawing on the work of Bettelheim, Erikson, Anna Freud and Lewin (all German Jews), Sarnoff sees adult maladaption (which he labels Jewish anti-Semitism) as a direct result of childhood insecurity. This was yet another attempt to create categories of "healthy" and "diseased" Jews based, as with Lewin and Bettelheim, on social rather than biological causes. The problem with Sarnoff and all of the other psychologists and sociologists who followed this model for "self-hatred" is that they made specific assumptions about what is "healthy" and what is "sick." To label entire categories of identity as "diseased" is to indulge in the type of polemic that lies behind the very concept of self-hatred, for, as has been shown, the double bind of identity formations may have a productive as well as a destructive outcome.

What is more, the strict polar definition of identity implied by the label "self-hatred" rests on a specific set of historical presuppositions about the structure of identity. This German model, if one may so label it, sees a simple and direct relationship between the internalization of a negative image of the Jew and the resultant shaping of the Jew's identity. This was valid within a culture that postulated an absolute polarity between "German" and "Jew." The "Germans," since they did not exist as an entity, needed some means of defining their fictional homogeneity. They did so by defining it negatively. We are Germans, which means that we are not Jews. This definition existed within Germany as a powerful and unbridgeable abyss between the fiction of the homogeneity of the "German" people and the assigned role of the Jew as the litmus test of difference. Once it became evident to the German Jews of the late nineteenth century that they had fallen into the double bind of this self-definition, they attempted to postulate other models for their own identity. These models were often simply negations or adaptions of the anti-Semitic image of the Jew. Either the Eastern Jew became the idealized image of the Jew, but an image shaped out of the fictions of Western Jewry, or the Eastern Jew remained as the antithesis of the healthy Jew. In defining and sharpening the idea of self-hatred as a category of illness,

German Jews were able to relegate those Jews viewed as unsuccessful in their adaptation to a separate class, the diseased. They incorporated into this category all of the negative qualities with which they were labeled and from which they wished to distance themselves. The protean category of the self-hating Jew was thus developed. It placed the "bad" Jews within an accepted and recognized category of the anti-Semitic science of race, the psychopathology of the Jew, and separated them from the Jewish identity of the observer.

The "insane" Jew, the Jewish self-hater, was defined within a world in which there were specific limits on the concept of difference. When this concept emigrated to the United States, before and during the Holocaust, clothed in the status of German science, it was adopted without any question—this in a society in which the complexity of the definition of difference eliminated any simple polar definition of the Jew. Even though the myth of the "hidden language" of the Jews existed in American anti-Semitism, there was already a central racial marker for difference in the United States: the black. Class distinctions in the United States had more to do with defining difference for the Jew than did racial distinctions. Because of this, the very concept of the "Jew" as a label for difference was fragmented, especially after the Holocaust and the establishment of the state of Israel.

But most important was the power of myth. In defining difference, the Germans defined themselves as monolithically German until 1945. This was the central myth about the definition of German identity. It had nothing to do with reality; if anything, it attempted to transcend the realities of a pluralistic group, itself politically and culturally fragmented. The central myth of twentieth-century America, especially after the Second World War, was the myth of American heterogeneity—not the melting pot but the ability to possess multiple identities. The power of this myth, itself fraught with the potential of the double bind, undermined the definition of the "self-hating Jew" within the model provided by German psychology. This model, based on valid psychological principles such as identification and projection, nevertheless reflected its historical origins. When applied to the American Jewish experience, it provided a working label for the signification of specific modes of divergence, modes that eventually turned upon the ideological implications of "Jewish self-hatred." For "self-hatred" among Jews is not the special prerogative of any specific group of Jews: It is the result of the internalized contrast between any society in which the possibility of acceptance is extended to any marginal group and the projection of the negative image of this group onto a fiction of itself that leads to "self-hatred" of self-abnegation. The German experience of the early twentieth century localized this general psychological truth in the experience of the assimilated Jew in Germany and thus endowed the overall experience of projection and identification with a specific ideological bias. Within all worlds of privilege this pattern repeats itself, but always with specific historical variations. The development of the concept of self-hatred within the experience of German Jewry led to a narrowing of the focus of the concept and to its interpretation within the specific contours of German Jewish experience. It was the tension between this more rigid, limited understanding of self-hatred (with its concomitant glorification of the difference of the Jew) and the post-Holocaust experience in the United States that provided yet another double bind through the American perception of Jewish identity formation after the Holocaust.

II

This double bind is worked out in great detail in Henry Bean's film *The Believer.* It is a powerful evocation of the legacy of the Shoah as filtered through a post-Holocaust, American sensibility. This story (or perhaps better this fantasy) about the impact of the memory of the Shoah on a young man in his twenties in contemporary America presents a perfect example of "identification with the aggressor." Anna Freud had already coined this term in 1936 in Vienna. When she came to work in London with children rescued from Nazi Europe after 1939, she described how these Jewish children when they played war games identified the warring factions as "Nazis and Jews." And all of the children wanted to be Nazis. She tied this behavior to a means of defending the integrity of the "ego," of that part of our psyche that defines our identity. She sees the children as identifying with the successful Nazis and rejecting their identity as the inevitable Jewish victims. This she links to the ultimate form of aggression against the self, suicide. A recent example of this "identification with the aggressor" is to be found in an autobiographical essay by the

Moscow writer Alexander Gelman, a Jew who survived the Nazi ghetto at Bershad:

> I went mad at the age of eight.
>
> They were real German units, albeit under my personal command. For my games I used the real military forces moving on that road. I would turn them this way and that to suit my plans....
>
> Did I understand that I was a Jew, that everyone there was Jewish and that was why we were being punished? Yes, I did. But in my games I stopped being Jewish. There were no Jews in them—no Jews served in my troops, there was not a single Jew on my staff. I only became Jewish in intervals between battles, like an actor stepping out of character for a while. I realize now that my games saved me. If today I am more or less sane it is thanks to the fact that—like a madman—I never stopped playing. I played ceaselessly through those three years, and continued playing for a long time following my return, after the war.

Being Jewish here means being the victim and, therefore, being marked for destruction, something that no "ego" can easily accept. For our bottom line is that we must preserve ourselves psychologically at all costs, even through becoming that force that wishes to destroy us.

When we first meet Danny Balint (played by Canadian actor Ryan Gosling) in *The Believer* we see him only as a neo-Nazi thug in the ultimate "Jewish" city, New York, who seems truly to enjoy beating up Jews as well as railing against the "international Jewish conspiracy." Only slowly in the course of the film do we learn his secret. Through the agency of a reporter (played by Garret Dillahunt) we begin to unravel Danny's background, to discover that he had been raised an Orthodox Jew. Indeed the moment of true revelation comes in the confrontation with the reporter in a diner, where Danny eventually pulls out a gun. We initially believe that it is to threaten the reporter into keeping quiet. Yet, following Anna Freud's model, he puts the gun to his own head, quite out of keeping with his neo-Nazi identity, and threatens to commit suicide if the reporter prints the fact that he is a Jew. For "identification with the aggressor" is simply an attenuated form of suicide.

Already as a child Danny Balint had begun to question his Jewish identity because of his internalizing Jewish victimhood in the Shoah. Being "Jewish" for him means, in the first order, being a victim, and that is something he truly "never again" wants Jews to experience. His answer to his overwhelming, American identification with the Holocaust as the defining moment that shaped his Jewish identity is to become one of the perpetrators, to join, and indeed to inspire a neo-Nazi cult. Smarter than all of the others in the group, he quickly becomes their leader and spokesman. Only in the course of the violence and murders that they undertake and his confrontation with the reporter who knows his secret does his Jewish identity reappear. By the end of the film he becomes a martyr to his own identification with the Jews as the victims of his own plots, dying in a bombing that he has instigated.

In earlier films on the Shoah, from Alain Renais's *Night and Fog* (1956) to Claude Lanzmann's *Shoah* (1985) to Steven Spielberg's *Schindler's List* (1993), the line between victim and perpetrator, between Jew and Nazi, is absolute.[1] These films provide a trajectory in the means of imaging the Holocaust in the cinema. They move from the image of the Shoah in which the victims are literally missing or present as photographs from the liberation of the camps to accounts in which living survivors provide narratives of the past (and in the case of Spielberg's film accounts of their meaningful survival). *The Believer* provides a further account of the third generation of Jews in America after the Holocaust. They were not only spared the direct confrontation with the Shoah because of its isolation in the United States, but now, two generations later, a generation that has the experience of the Shoah as a narrative that shapes the American Jewish collective identity in the twenty-first century.[2]

How can such a film succeed in capturing an aspect of the Shoah as imagined in American society in which Jews are an "over-represented minority" because they have become economically successful and thus part of the mainstream? The focus of the film is on the radical racist fringe in contemporary America in which anti-Semitism still exists as a potent force. This too is a reality on the American political landscape, if a peripheral one, but the impact of this fringe presence is extraordinary in shaping the protagonist's sense that he can move to the "other side" and be safe. He can become a perpetrator because the neo-Nazi movement is so marginal, so pathetic in those it recruits that a "smart Jew" could quickly become a leader.

This notion of "Jewish superior intelligence" must be understood as an aspect of the question of Jewish visibility in post-Shoah American cinema. How are Jews imagined to look in the cinema after the Shoah? Given the stereotype of the weak, pasty-faced Jewish intellectual that haunts films such as *The Young Lions* (1958), where Montgomery Clift seems to be the neurotic Jew incarnate, Danny Balint's incarnation as a tattooed skinhead presents the antithesis of his image as a Jewish school child. The tough neo-Nazi is the answer to the weak but smart Jew. Yet Jews after the Shoah come to assume a new type of body. Perhaps the classic case is the casting of Paul Newman (blue eyes, Jewish father, raised as a Christian Scientist) as the Jewish hero of the film based on Leon Uris's novel *Exodus* (1960) was one of the anomalies of this anxiety about the implied difference of American Jews. How could Jews be "racially" different as the Nazis (and neo-Nazis) claimed if they looked like Paul Newman! Indeed, in Robert Mandel's *School Ties* (1992) the theme of "passing" works only because of the sports activities of Brandon Frasier. He is not quite able to "pass" in the snooty (and anti-Semitic) private school that he attends. Yet in *School Ties* the character is not only athletic but also smart and compassionate. His athlete's body is not sufficient, within the narrative of the film, to enable him to be accepted, to pass successfully. Likewise the powerful, muscular body of Danny Balint attempts to mask the "Jew within," the pathetic, weak Jew as the victim.[3]

Neo-Nazis may be strong but they are also stupid or ineffectual, as *The Believer* shows. After the Shoah, Germans of all symbolic stripe come to embody a demonic quality, but certainly not intelligence. For their genius is that of the demented, evil intelligence—Moriarity to the smart Jew's Sherlock Holmes. Orson Welles in *The Stranger* (1946), Sam Jaffe as "the professor" in *The Asphalt Jungle* (1950), Peter Sellers as Dr. Merkwuerdigliebe in Stanley Kubrick's *Dr. Strangelove* (1964), Hardy Krüger in *Flight of the Phoenix* (1965), or, indeed, Walter Slezak or George Sanders in any of their fiendish Nazi incarnations in the "B" movies made before 1945 are "evil." Indeed, before *Exodus,* smart Jews, if they are not victims, could be the equivalent of the "evil" German. Such an image of the smart yet destructive Jew can be found in Frederick Wiseman's character as a nihilist-anarchist in *Viva Zapata!* (1952), leading the Mexican children of nature to their doom, apparently for the sheer pleasure of it.

Danny Balint identifies with the neo-Nazis spiritually as well as physically. He becomes a neo-Nazi in act and deed. Henry Bean noted upon accepting the Sundance Festival's Grand Jury Prize that "this is truly a story of love and hate. I love the provocative aspects...the notion of being a Jew and a Nazi at the same time." And yet this very aspect turns the film into a comment on the need for this type of identification among contemporary American Jews. The horror of this film lies as much in the presence of neo-Nazis in American society as in Danny Balint's "conversion" into a Nazi. But the slow unfolding of Danny's identity is the key to our understanding of what impact the Shoah can have on young American Jews raised in a world in which their identity is shaped by the narrative of the Holocaust. Self-hatred, with all of its history, takes on a new and forbidding face.

Notes

1. See especially Tony Barta, "Film Nazis: The Great Escape" in Tony Barta, ed., Screening the Past: Film and the Representation of History (Westport, CT: Praeger, 1998), pp. 127-48; Yosefa Loshitzky, ed., Spielberg's Holocaust (Bloomington: Indiana University Press, 1997); Stephen Lewis, Art Out of Agony: The Holocaust Theme in Literature, Sculpture and Film (Toronto: CBC Enterprises, 1984). See also Dominick LaCapra, History and Memory after Auschwitz (Ithaca, NY: Cornell University Press, 1998; Ilan Avisar, "Holocaust Movies and the Politics of Collective Memory," in Alvin H. Rosenfeld, ed., Thinking about the Holocaust: After Half a Century (Bloomington, IN: Indiana University Press, 1997), pp. 38-58; Janet Lungstrum, "Foreskin Fetishism: Jewish Male Difference in Europa, Europa," Screen 39 (1998): 53-66; Morris Zyrl and Saul S. Friedman, "The Holocaust as Seen in the Movies. A Handbook of Criticism, History, and Literary Writings," in Saul S. Friedman and Dennis Klein, eds., Holocaust Literature (Westport, CT: Greenwood, 1993), pp. 604-22.

2. Peter Novick, The Holocaust in American Life (New York: Houghton Mifflin, 1999).

3. See Sander L. Gilman, Smart Jews: The Construction of the Idea of Jewish Superior Intelligence at the Other End of the Bell Curve (The Inaugural Abraham Lincoln Lectures) (Lincoln: University of Nebraska Press, 1996).

Contributors

BETH PINSKER is the editor in chief of *The Independent.*

DAVID KRAEMER is Professor of Talmud and Rabbinics at the Jewish Theological Seminary of America. He is also a Senior Associate at CLAL, the National Jewish Center for Learning and Leadership.

SANDER L. GILMAN is a distinguished professor of the Liberal Arts and Medicine at the University of Illinois in Chicago and the director of the Humanities Laboratory. A cultural and literary historian, he is the author or editor of over sixty books.

HENRY BEAN

Novels:

False Match   Poseidon Press (Simon & Schuster), 1982
Emphasizing The Negative (nearing completion)
The Elevation of Strange Thoughts (far from completion)

Produced Screenplays:

Showboat	1988 Independent, 1977; director: Rick Schmidt
Heartaches	Canada, 1981; director: Don Shebib
Running Brave	Touchstone, 1982; director: Don Shebib
Internal Affairs	Paramount, 1990; director: Mike Figgis
Deep Cover	New Line, 1992; director: Bill Duke
Mulholland Falls	MGM, 1995; director: Lee Tamahouri
Desperate Measures	Sony/Tristar, 1997; director: Barbet Schroeder
Enemy of the State	Disney, 1998; director: Tony Scott
Foolproof	Castle Rock, 2001; director: Barbet Schroeder

Unproduced Screenplays:
(partial list)

Hard Feelings (with Leora Barish)
Basic Instinct 2 (with Leora Barish)
The Death & Life of Bobby Z
The Donner Party (with Mark Jacobson)
The Mitchell Brothers
Who You Know
Up (with Leora Barish)
Mickey's Monkey
Eldorado (with Leora Barish)

Writer/Director:

Thousand, (Fuller Films, 1997; 13 minutes); study for feature film.
The Believer, (Seven Arts/Fireworks, 2001)